Going On For God:

Encouraging the Next Generation to Grow Up and Go On For God.

A practical conversation for both
Christian parents <u>and</u> church leaders

by Mel Walker

Learn more about this book and its author by visiting
www.GoingOnForGod.com and
www.overboardministries.com

©Copyright 2018 by Mel Walker

This title is available for your favorite eReader.

Find other books by Overboard Ministries at
www.overboardministries.com. Comments or requests for publishing or
for Overboard Ministries information should be sent to
overboard@overboardministries.com.

ISBN 13: 978-1-943635-17-7
Published by Overboard Ministries 2018
All rights reserved.
Traverse City, Michigan

Cover design by Tim Schade: schadesnj@gmail.com

CONTENTS

Dedication

To Our Kids
—Kristi, Todd, and Travis—
the next generation of Walkers.

I pray every day for you that you will
keep going on for God.

Your Mom and I are so proud of you—
especially for your personal commitment to Christ,
His Word, and His work.

*"I have no greater joy than this, to hear of my children
walking in the truth."* 3 John 4

Acknowledgements

A page of acknowledgements will never do justice and can never include everyone who helped me in the production of this book, but I want to especially thank the following people for their involvement in this project:

- My wife and family—Thank you for your patience and encouragement—and thanks for going on this journey with me!
- Chris Woodward—Thanks for proofreading my manuscript. I greatly appreciate your help.
- Tim Schade—Thanks so much for your lasting friendship with me and our family, and your amazing work as the graphic artist and designer of the book cover, graphics, and promotional materials for this ministry. It's always great working with you.
- Chris Brown—Thank you for your assistance and great ideas on my website (www.GoingOnForGod.com) and for serving as my personal "tech expert." Thanks too for serving on the board of Vision For Youth.
- Joe Castaneda & Overboard—Your support and partnership in publishing this book is much appreciated. Let's keep doing projects together.
- Lyndsey Brown—Thanks so much for working with me again on another book project. I get it that editors exist to make writers look good. You do that very well!
- Tim Ahlgrim—Thanks for contributing the article in the Appendix of this book, and thanks for your faithful ministry with Vision For Youth.

Preface

Dear Readers,

I want to begin with a very personal and heartfelt note to my readers. The theme of this book has become the central focus of my life and ministry. I am absolutely convinced that my life's mission is to encourage members of the next generation to grow up and go on for God.

Of course, this passion begins with our own children—and continues now with our grandchildren. Our kids are now all adults, but Peggy and I pray every day for our grandkids that they will each come to Christ, grow in Him, and then live faithfully for the Lord throughout the course of their lives. It would break my heart if members of our family chose to walk away from God when they became adults.

This desire continues to all the young people of the next generation, particularly those who have been a part of my ministries over the years. As someone who has dedicated his life to youth ministry, I understand the joys and the sorrows of working with kids in church youth groups or other youth ministry endeavors because I am old enough to have seen a few different generations grow up from childhood into adulthood. The Lord has given me a great burden for them as well. I pray specifically that every lesson I teach, every message I speak, every paragraph I write, and every event I plan will be greatly used by God to impact lives of the next generation. I don't want them to walk away from God either.

That is exactly why I begin the first conversation in this book by asking Christian parents and church leaders alike, "What do we want for our kids?" Hopefully and prayerfully, we all can answer that we want them to grow in Christ and to go on for Him throughout their adult lives!

Of course, I am a champion of God's *amazing* grace. We are saved by His grace and we can live the Christian life only by His grace. That is my personal story; and let me say emphatically that God's grace is the pivotal point of your story as well. I understand that some readers will see the title of this book and its basic premise as a frustration or as a discouragement because they have family members or friends, or they know and love young people, who have walked away from God and His work. I get it that there are many heartbreaking accounts out there. I hurt for those readers with loved ones in this stage of life. Please remember that their story is not finished yet. God is still on His throne and He is still in the business of claiming and reclaiming lost souls. This book is not intended to be a formula or recipe for producing perfect kids! We all need the strength and encouragement that comes from God doing only what God can do. He can bring *prodigals* back to Himself. That's what His grace is all about.

My 40-plus years of active involvement in various aspects of youth ministry, and especially my efforts in working on this book have led me to the conviction that impacting emerging generations is essential for both Christian families **and** the church. As Christ followers, we each have the responsibility to reproduce our faith in the lives of the next generation. As Christ tarries before His return, we have the Biblical mandate to impact generation after generation. Biblical truth and a consistent Christian life were designed by God to be taught to and caught by our kids—and I'm saying that both to parents and pastors and other church leaders. They are *our* kids, and we must take the responsibility to intentionally encourage them for long-term spiritual maturity.

That being said, there are some foundational terms or phrases I use repetitively in this book which require some explanation and definition.

Inter-generational – I have hyphenated this word to draw attention to the idea of developing healthy and growing relationships between adults and younger people. I understand that others may refer to multi-generational or cross-generational connections, but I like the idea of the prefix "inter," which according to Dictionary.com implies "between, among, in the midst of, mutually, reciprocally, or together."[1] In other words, I use this term repeatedly to make the case that we need the generations to actually connect and develop meaningful relationships, not just mingle.

Emerging adults or emerging generations – I originally borrowed this idea from Jeffrey Arnett's work *Emerging Adulthood: The Winding Road from the Late Teens Through the Twenties.* I use these terms most often to describe the lengthening transition from childhood into adulthood.

Youth ministry – This term resonates with me more than the currently more popular *"student ministry"* only because I see today's young people as having more roles and more responsibilities than just as students in a particular educational setting. Teenagers and young adults are people; they are human beings with many more functions and relationships than as students only.

Youth group – Likewise I use this expression to describe teenagers collectively gathering together in a variety of settings and programs in a ministry established and developed in and through a local church. I understand that some see this term as having negative connotations that somehow imply an exclusive membership of insiders only, where visitors and other outsiders are not welcome. That is not my intent in any way in this book. I use *"youth group"* to refer to a church's overall ministry to teenagers.

Traditional churches – I do not use the word *"traditional"* here to necessarily describe outdated or old-fashioned churches that no longer meet the needs of their communities. I use the term *"traditional churches"* to refer to churches that seem to organize their ministries and programs in the same ways as most other churches have done. For instance, I use this word to describe churches that still employ age-segregated methodology exclusively, which the readers of my last book *Inter-Generational Youth Ministry: Why a Balanced View of Connecting the Generations is Essential for The Church* will realize I am not a fan of that particular approach.

Conversation – You will notice right away I have named the individual section headers "conversations" instead of the more common delineation of "chapters." That was my choice because I hope this book will launch a dialogue with Christian parents, pastors, and other church leaders from a variety of backgrounds and individual situations. What specifically are we doing to encourage long-term spiritual growth in our kids? This topic is so important that we must not leave it to chance or circumstance. Let's help each other think this through.

Thanks, readers for taking the time to read through this preface and my introductory comments about this book.

Committed to impacting the next generation,
-Mel

Introduction

Do you know this kid?

He grew up in a Christian home and was active in church activities since he was young. His parents loved the Lord and made church a top priority. This young man was mentored by committed Christian leaders who demonstrated faithfulness and spiritual maturity. In fact, his mentors were some of the leading voices in the church. He attended prayer meetings as a boy; and later as a young man, he actively participated in a short-term missions trip.

Obviously, he was on a spiritual success trajectory, right? His future was bright and his potential for ministry success seemed sure. But, then something happened. We are not sure what exactly, but there was a failure of some sort. He stopped serving, he quit the ministry, and went back home. Church leaders were devastated and confused. Some of the leaders wanted to encourage him and get him some help. Others separated from him and viewed him as a quitter.

This kid, with the once incredibly bright future, who was actively involved in everything the church had to offer, was now a failure and a drop out.

You know him, don't you? Or at least you've known someone with a story very similar to his. This story seems very contemporary, and it sounds like this could be the prototype for today's church dropout statistics. Church kids, once very active in church and youth group, are dropping out from active involvement in church. Yep, we know this story. It could have happened in my church or your church.

But, this story is actually from the Bible! It happened over two thousand years ago. The kid's name was John Mark, and his story is told to us in Acts 12 through 15. Take a few moments right now to read the narrative in your copy of the Scriptures.

We learn that John Mark grew up in church. The early church met in his parents' house. He attended the all-night prayer meeting when the Apostle Peter showed up after God miraculously helped him escape from prison. John Mark was mentored by some of the most prominent church leaders of his time like Barnabas, Peter, and the Apostle Paul. Plus, John Mark was selected to go along with some of these great mentors on the very first missions trip ever.

His path to the future seemed secure. But his course changed. He became a ministry dropout. We're not sure exactly why it happened, but John Mark deserted his coworkers and went back home. His departure even became a point of contention between the veteran members of the missions team, Saul (soon to be renamed Paul) and Barnabas. Barnabas wanted to continue investing his life in young John Mark. He saw potential and wanted to get him some help, training, and encouragement. But, Saul saw things differently. He viewed John Mark as a quitter—as a deserter and a failure.

This disagreement cased such a rift between these experienced ministry leaders that their team was blown apart—Barnabas taking his young cousin off to Cyprus, undoubtedly to reconnect with Peter; and Saul finding Silas as a replacement.

So, what became of John Mark? How did his story end? Did this kid with so much ministry potential end up as the consummate drop-out, or were other factors in play that changed his course?

You probably know the ending.

Young John Mark grew up to go on for God! In fact, the Apostle Paul, who earlier didn't want anything to do with this quitter, writes (2 Timothy 4:11), *"John Mark...is useful to me for ministry."* And, he was. Not only did Paul view John Mark as a ministry success story, so did the Lord. So much so, that this same young man was ultimately used by God to be the human author of one of the books of the Bible—the Gospel of Mark.

This kid with the potential for a phenomenal ministry future became a quitter, a drop out. And yet, God continued to work in John Mark's life. Some ministry veterans confronted him and labeled him as a deserter. Other Christian leaders encouraged him and didn't let him fall off of the proverbial spiritual shelf. He ended up as a success story as someone greatly used by God for eternal impact.

He grew up to go on for God!

This book is all about helping other young people do that too. We'll use the story of John Mark here as a visual aid for today's young people. You probably know kids with stories very similar to his. Others will have vastly different storylines. But, our objective must be the same. We want to reach the next generation for Christ and then help them grow up toward spiritual maturity.

The Biblical narrative of John Mark[2] can serve as our launching pad to encourage other young people to grow up, perhaps go through difficult life experiences, and continue growing in Christ. Some of the influences in John Mark's life can help us with this process today. This book will seek to identify some of the influences God used in the life of John Mark and other relevant principles as catalysts for intentional action steps for Christian parents and church leaders today.

But first we'll take a look at a clear Biblical objective for helping and encouraging today's young people to grow up and go on for God. Plus, we'll take a brief look at the current state of the family and the church.

Let's have a conversation about it.

*"For what is our hope, or joy, or crown of rejoicing? Is it not even **you** in the presence of our Lord Jesus Christ at His coming?"*
1 Thessalonians 2:19

Coversation #1
What Do We Want For Our Kids?

"Children grow up!"

I often make this declaration when presenting training workshops for Christian parents and church leaders. I somewhat facetiously tell the participants that this simple, quite obvious fact may be the most profound statement I have ever made.

Certainly, we know it to be true. But I am convinced that there are many parents and church leaders alike who are so concerned with *now* that a long-term view of maturity can be lost in the immediate reality of what is necessary at the moment. We want our children to grow up and we want them to mature in all aspects of their lives. However, the pressing, current matters of life often crowd out the enduring end result of what we want for our children. Spiritually speaking, we want them to grow up and go on for God! We don't want them to stay locked in a Peter Pan existence of eternal childhood. We want them to grow into mature adults. And we want them to grow up to be Godly!

So, I want to begin this book by emphatically saying that this process demands intentionality—both from Christian parents and the church!

Many years ago I had an experience I will never forget. As a young youth pastor, I was called to make an emergency visit to a local children's hospital because of an accident affecting one of the children from our church. This was my first trip to this sprawling, university-based medical complex, and I took a wrong turn somewhere along my journey and ended up in the wrong room. I expected to find the young man and his family; but instead I saw a cold, sterile hospital crib in the center of room. The crib's occupant was a baby who was hooked up to several monitors by a series of wires and tubes. My heart was broken as I looked at this child who obviously had a very serious medical condition.

Just then a team of doctors and nurses entered the room. That particular hospital system required visiting ministers to wear clip-on name tags with the word "Clergy" clearly printed in large letters. The staff was helpful and pointed me in the right direction, and I soon found the correct room. Just before leaving, I took the opportunity to ask what was wrong with the child.

What they told me has stuck in my mind ever since—and what I saw that day is still one of the saddest experiences of my entire life. The baby in that crib was almost eight years old, but had not grown in any area of his life. He would never grow like other children. Although alive, with breathing capacity and a heartbeat, this child would never grow up. Even writing about it now makes me sad, and I have a deep sense of sympathy and pain for that child and his family.

I believe it is even sadder for children to not grow up spiritually—if they do not come to Christ (as the Bible puts it, to be *"born again"*—see John 3:7), grow in Him, and then ultimately go on for God. That's why the truth of Ephesians 4:15 and 16 is so important: *"That we should no longer be children, tossed to and fro and carried about with every wind of doctrine, by the trickery of men, in the cunning craftiness of deceitful plotting, but, speaking the truth in love, may grow up in all things into Him who is the head—Christ."*

The broader context of this section in Ephesians 4 is about the purpose of the church. It's clear from this passage that God wants His followers to grow into spiritual maturity. He doesn't want us remain as spiritual babies—and He gave us His church[3] to help us grow up and go on for God.

This passage can be considered as a Biblical foundation on which to build our thinking on what Christ's church is to accomplish. This includes reaching people for Christ, and then discipling and teaching them to become mature in their relationship with Christ.

There's another equally revealing passage in the same Epistle that emphasizes this growth process. Let's take a look at Ephesians 6:1-4, especially verse 4. In this text, Christian parents, particularly fathers, are to *"bring them up in the training and admonition of the Lord."* Here too, spiritual maturity is the end result. Notice there is another God-ordained institution in place for that to happen. The context of the first few verses in Ephesians 6 is about parents. Christian parents must be about the business of helping their children grow in spiritual maturity.

Both institutions (the church and the Christian home) must be committed to helping children grow so that they live for God as adults! It is obvious from the text that God does not want His followers to remain as children.

This is a book then about the mutual objective these two God-given institutions have in common for the on-going, spiritual benefit of our young people. This is not necessarily a book on parenting, but I honestly believe all Christian parents should read it and implement its principles. Likewise, this is not a book on church structure either, but I also believe all church leaders would benefit from reading this book and thinking through how to address these matters in their local churches.

I am not claiming to be a parenting expert, but after spending most of my working life with young people and after talking with scores of parents, I have witnessed these concerns firsthand. I care deeply about the church **and** the family and I am very passionate about those two God-given institutions working together for the long-term benefit of emerging generations.

Over the course of this book project, the Lord gave me the opportunity to visit about 70 different churches, sometimes as a guest speaker and sometimes just as a visitor. These experiences have given me an insider's perspective of some of the current trends and issues facing both Christian families and churches in today's postmodern, post-Christian, and post-church culture. In addition, the Lord has given me over 40 years of experience in various aspects of youth ministry, including positions as a youth pastor, Christian college professor and administrator, editor and writer of church youth materials, and as an author of youth ministry related books. Plus, I am a parent of now adult children and a grandparent. God has used these various experiences to put a growing burden on my heart to encourage Godly parents and church leaders to team up to help children grow up and go on for God.

In many ways, this book is designed be a follow-up volume to my earlier work *Inter-Generational Youth Ministry: Why a Balanced View of Connecting the Generations is Essential for The Church.*[4] In that book I argue that developing inter-generational relationships is imperative for the church. Young people need older people, and likewise older people need young people. My focus here is that Christian parents and the church must be absolutely committed to the spiritual maturity of emerging generations.[5]

In a very real sense, my work in this book is the outgrowth of a true inter-generational philosophy. Christian families need the consistency and reinforcement that the larger body of Christ (His Church) provides, and the church needs the stability and collaboration of Godly families. These two institutions must work together and be on the same page, for the same purpose.

By saying this, I am not downplaying the personal responsibility believers have individually, working within the power of Christ and the Holy Spirit, to grow closer to Christ on their own. Personal growth is obviously very, very important for every individual Christ follower. We see this in Scripture passages like 1 Corinthians 11:1, Ephesians 5:1-2, Philippians 2:5, 1 Thessalonians 1:6, 1 Timothy 4:7, and 1 John 3:7.

But, I want to be very clear here. **The top priority** for Christian parents and for the church is to see the next generation come to Christ, mature in Him, and then continue living for God. And both institutions must be intentional. As proclaimed by Biblical scholar, educator, and writer, Dr. Charles Ryrie, "The home and the church are the **only** two God-ordained 'institutions' for carrying out His work."[6] "Carrying out His work" here doesn't just mean The Great Commission (Matthew 28:18-20, Mark 16:15, Luke 24:46-48, Acts 1:8), though obviously it includes that. But it also means, if I can borrow from the oft-quoted Bill Hybels, that both the church and parents are to develop "fully devoted followers of Christ."[7] It's so important for our kids to grow into maturity in Christ. The future is at stake. Our children will grow up into adulthood physically—and they'll do it with or without Godly influences. I argue for the Godly influences.

I frequently tell audiences when I speak that I didn't care if my children grew up to be "successful" in the eyes of today's secular culture. But, my wife and I were very, very concerned that they grew up to be Godly! If that's our motive, if that's our objective, then we must be intentional about the process.

Children *will* grow up!

"But know this …perilous times will come…" 2 Timothy 3:1

Conversation #2
A Cause for Concern: Are the Church and the Family In Trouble?

There was a day when the two most stable institutions in culture were the family and the church. My generation came of age during those seemingly idyllic times. The family was considered as the bedrock of our society. It seemed as if most people aspired to get married at a young age and then have children relatively soon. This was considered the norm, and maybe even the ideal. American culture was dominated by the traditional family. Likewise, the church was often seen as central to community life. Many parents realized the importance of taking their kids to church. But things changed.

The State of the Family

I grew up in an *Ozzie and Harriett, Father Knows Best,* and *Leave It To Beaver* world. "The family loomed so large in America's psyche," wrote New York Times columnist Bernard Weinraub about the long-running sitcom *The Adventures of Ozzie and Harriet*.[8] Television, if not culture as a whole, was dominated by the so-called "nuclear family" of two married parents (most often white, Anglo-Saxon Americans), where the father worked outside of the home, the mother was a stay-at-home housewife, and there were children living at home.[9] Indeed, the family unit in those days was seen as the nucleus or core of society.

In just a few short decades, American culture's appetite for comedic television had switched from family-oriented themes to shows like *Friends* and *Seinfeld*—programs that weren't about the family unit at all.[10] It was almost as if the family unit had been systematically, maybe even deliberately, replaced. And frankly, contemporary culture's war on family values has only made things worse since then.

A look at the present-day roster of television's situation comedies and the American family perhaps reveals another cultural shift. Recent viewing choices include TV shows such as *Modern Family,* a program that "embodies the richly diverse definition of family now held by contemporary Americans,"[11] and the reappearance of *Will and Grace,* another sitcom that was recognized as "helping and improving public opinion of the LGBT community."[12]

The growing popularity of these "family" shows illustrate that the basic definition of family is certainly changing.[13] In fact, these headlines from recent internet news feeds caught my attention: "Zoning Dispute Causes Debate Over Definition of Family"[14] and "Department Of Labor Revises Definition Of 'Spouse' Under The Family And Medical Leave Act To Expand Rights To All Same-Sex Couples."[15]

It seems the nucleus of the American culture is changing literally before our eyes. George Barna and David Kinnaman of the Barna Research Group agree: "Marriage is being redefined in America. The growing acceptance of divorce and serial marriage, the embrace of cohabitation, and increasing skepticism about marriage in general all have an impact on what's considered 'normal' when it comes to the family."[16]

As an observer of cultural trends, I must admit that I have some very real concerns about the state of marriage and the family in today's culture. A recent Barna Group study on the characteristics of "Gen Z" (the current generation of young people in the US) made this claim: "This is the first time a generation has not selected 'family' as the top factor in their sense of self."[17] It's very revealing to realize that a growing number of kids today do not see "the family" as one of the most important things in their lives.

The family structure permeates Scripture: from Adam and Eve, to the Jewish Nation, to the examples of Godly families in the New Testament. But the Bible records plenty of examples of dysfunctional families as well.[18] Yes, look around and you will see the God-ordained institution of the family to be struggling. It seems as if dysfunctional families and other living scenarios are more the norm today than are solid, traditional families.

Here are some of the newer trends facing marriage and family living:

- According to the American Psychological Association, 40 to 50 percent of marriages in the United States end in divorce; and the divorce rate for subsequent marriages is even higher. [19]
- "[Millennials] are the first generation being born primarily out of wedlock, with a high percentage being raised by single parents or in other non-traditional arrangements."[20]
- "Roughly six-in-ten adults younger than 35 are now living without a spouse or partner," up significantly from just 10 years ago.[21]
- In 1960, the average age of people getting married was about 21.[22] According to recent US Census Bureau statistics, the current average age of marriage has risen to over 27. [23]
- More than 12 million moms and dads are raising their children alone in the United States.[24]
- Recent research has revealed more single parents are sharing children, more gay and lesbian couples are raising children, and more 20-something and 30-something singles are forming de facto households.[25]
- The U.S. Supreme Court (in June 2015) ruled there is a federal constitutional right to same-sex marriage. The Court's sweeping ruling has the net effect of legalizing same-sex marriage at the federal and state levels across the entire country. The ruling effectively negates 31 state marriage amendments plus other states' laws safeguarding man/woman marriage, and requires every state to license and recognize same-sex marriages.[26]

Certainly, local church ministries are being affected by these contemporary statistics and trends. It is my contention that more than ever the church will need to be *"a family"* — accepting of and ministering to a growing number of people in modern culture who do not fit into traditional marriage and family structures. (More about this trend will be discussed later in the book.) This **does not** mean that we need to acquiesce to the sinful practices of society. (Read Romans 1:18-32 and 2 Timothy 3:1-9.) It **does** mean that the church must figure out how to reach out to an ever-changing cultural demographic.

The State of the Church

The church in the 21st century is likewise facing a time of crisis. Once a key building block of culture, church involvement or even simple church attendance in today's society has become blasé. Current research seems to substantiate this claim. According to recent figures, approximately 43% of American adults consider themselves "churchless"[27]—which is the highest percentage in United States history. However, other authors report realistic church attendance numbers to actually be significantly lower—maybe only around 20%.[28] The Hartford Institute for Religion Research revealed the median size of churches in the United States is about 75 people, which is down considerably from past records.[29] Other sources claim that even people who consider themselves to be active church-goers actually only rarely attend church.[30]

In simple terms, I think it's safe to conclude that participation in church has noticeably diminished over the last few decades.

One reason for the decline in church attendance may be due to how many young adults are leaving the church following high school graduation. A helpful source of information about this departure from church is *Essential Church: Reclaiming a Generation of Dropouts* by Thom Rainer and San Rainer III. They report the findings of a major study: "More than two-thirds of young churchgoing adults in America drop out of church between the ages of eighteen and twenty-two."[31] Much has been written about this scenario—why it is happening and what to do about it—but, the tendency for young adults to walk away from involvement in church has definitely contributed to overall decline in American churches.

Another factor that has led to the drop in attendance and participation in the local church is the rise of the "nones"[32] in this country. Paul Taylor, in an important book from the Pew Research Center, states, "The number of Americans who do not identify with any religion—the 'nones'—has been growing at a dramatic pace...Their ranks now include more than 13 million people who say they have no particular religious affiliation."[33]

This is explained in greater detail by James Emery White: "One-third of Americans under thirty say they have no religious affiliation, compared to 9 percent of those sixty-five and older. This is due to 'generational replacement' as a younger generation assumes the place of an older one that is decidedly more religious."[34]

Although I am not necessarily a fan of the title of Dan Kimball's book *They Like Jesus But Not The Church: Insights from Emerging Generations,* I do see the value in what he says about those in their late teens to thirties. Referencing the absence of the younger generations in church, he explains, "Generally it is the largest segment missing from most of our churches, and so as we look to the future of the church, it's an age group we really need to pay attention to...We need to rethink what we are doing as church leaders in a changing culture."[35]

Cause and Effect?

I hope readers understand that theologically speaking I am not a gloom-and-doom prognosticator who is predicting the imminent demise of the family or the church. The Bible makes it clear that neither institution is going away. For instance, in the Apostle Paul's classic discourse in Ephesians 5:22-33, the inspired Word of God is emphatic about the commitment Christ made with His church as an illustration of the union between husbands and wives. Both of these relationships (Christ and the church, as well as the bond between husbands and wives) are designed by God to last forever. Both of these institutions are God's idea, and He really didn't create a "Plan B."

I'm wondering, however, if the cultural decline of these two basic institutions has created a circular "cause and effect" situation in families, in the church, and in culture as a whole. Perhaps because Christian homes and so many churches are struggling, it has led to a scenario where the spiritual maturity of the next generation is at risk as well. To put it another way, if the home and the church were intentional and deliberate about their mutual objective of spiritual maturity, we would be developing more and more children, teenagers, and young adults who grow up and go on for God!

That's the basic idea presented in this book: the church and Godly parents are both responsible for the on-going spiritual health of our young people. But, how can this happen when these two foundational institutions seem to be in so much trouble?

Before we discuss some possible solutions, let's talk more about the mass exodus of young adults from the church.

"...that you may know how you ought to conduct yourself in the house of God, which is the church of the living God, the pillar and ground of truth." 1 Timothy 3:15

Conversation #3
Church Drop Outs: Why Are Young Adults Leaving and What Can We Do About It?

"Young adults aren't sticking with church."

That headline and the corresponding article in *USA Today* from a few years ago substantiated the data behind our fears. We've all heard that the number one time for people to quit going to church, and in fact to walk away from their relationship with God, is immediately following high school. This article, which was based on information gathered by LifeWay Research, shouted the facts: "Seven in 10 Protestants ages 18 to 30—both evangelical and mainline—who went to church regularly in high school said they quit attending by age 23."[36]

That article, along with other writers and researchers who cited similar church drop out statistics, became the launching pad for what became a multi-year journey for me. I believed the reports. The sources are too credible and too numerous not to accept the facts. Young adults, who were once active in youth group and church as kids, are leaving church in droves—and I wanted to know why.

As I mentioned previously, the Lord gave me the opportunity to visit about 70 different churches while I was working on this book. One church posted a membership of almost 15,000; another had an average attendance of 11 people. Most of the churches I visited were what could be called traditional churches, but I also took a look at house churches, so-called "mega-churches," church plants, a family-integrated church, and multi-site churches. Some of these churches were in large cities, some in suburbia, some in small communities, and others were out in the country. The churches were mainly Protestant (with the majority being Baptist or baptistic churches), while several others referred to themselves as non-denominational.

During my travels and during my other ministry involvements, I spoke with hundreds of young adults and church leaders alike and asked them about the much-publicized statistics like the 70 percent departure rate I quoted earlier. I asked them if their own experience mirrored that national average or if they were seeing something different. Overwhelmingly, the churches I visited had experienced comparable tendencies. My personal conversations definitely corroborated and supported the national trends. Many, many kids who were once very active in church youth group left the church when they became young adults.

The follow up question was obvious: Why? I asked them about the reasons why emerging generations would quit attending church. The following four reasons were listed by these young adults as the top explanations for the departure.

Reasons Young Adults Might Walk Away from Church

1. **<u>Young adults are more likely to leave church if they are not grounded in Biblical truth</u>.** My conversations with church leaders and young adults led me to the conclusion that the number one reason kids walk away from church is if they are not personally grounded in their faith. When children are young they usually go to church because their parents go. It is during "college age" (whether they are actually in school, working, or in the military—it doesn't matter), when most people question their faith. They wonder, "Do I really believe

this?" My discussions revealed that if they did not have a strong Biblical foundation for their beliefs, they were likely to be confused and insecure, and ultimately likely to walk away from church and even question their relationship with God. It's that serious. I think that's why a recent article in the New York Post described Millennials as "a generation still uncertain what it stands for." [37]

2. **Young adults are more likely to drop out of church if they do not have a sense of personal "ownership" in church.** Over and over again I heard from young adults, who had left regular involvement in church, that their experience in youth group featured entertainment and a consumeristic philosophy. In other words, the youth program in the churches they attended were characterized by "fun and games" and gave the teenagers "everything they wanted," but that model failed to produce long-term disciples of Christ. These young adults seemed to have fun when they were in youth group, and they had fond memories of the adult leaders who ran those programs, but they did not have a lasting affinity for the church as a whole.

3. **Young adults are more likely to quit going to church if they are not receiving consistent messages from influential adults.** Almost every young adult I spoke to talked about the adult "hypocrites" they knew when they were in youth group. Some of the people I interviewed knew church leaders with sinful habits of sexual immorality or financial impropriety, and they each mentioned adults who seemed to be judgmental and negative toward the teenagers in church. Plus, many of them told stories of adults who "preached" at teenagers not to be involved with "sinful" external behavior, but who did not demonstrate a genuine love for Christ in front of the teens. It was obvious—if the students did not have Godly, influential, and consistent

adults in their lives, they were much more likely to walk away. They did not want to stay involved in a church like that!

4. **Young adults are more likely to abandon church if they do not have interpersonal relationships with members of other generations in the church.** Many of the young adults who left churches did so because they really did not know many adults in the church. They knew a handful of youth leaders, and they knew the pastor and other church leaders, but really didn't have a very positive view of them. They seemed to enjoy youth group and appreciated the opportunity to get to know other kids who claimed Christ, but once they graduated from high school and were not welcome in youth group, the church really didn't have anything for them. They did not feel welcome in "big church" because they didn't know very many of the regular adults. Readers, let's face it—many of our churches do a lousy job of helping emerging adults transition into the overall life of the church.

Based upon those personal conversations and the four basic reasons I listed above about why young adults would walk away from church, I want to suggest a proactive strategy for pastors, youth workers, and other church leaders, and a corresponding approach for Christian parents to consider implementing in their own family practices that will address those four specific matters.

What Can Church Leaders Do to Help?

1. **Teach and preach the clear and complete exposition of Scripture and help young people apply Biblical principles to their own lives**. Our plan to keep emerging adults in church must start and end with the Gospel. It is the Word of God that changes people's lives (see Hebrews 4:12 and Romans 12:1-2), and it is the Bible that

moves Christ followers in the process toward Christ-likeness (see 2 Corinthians 3:18 and 2 Peter 3:14-18). I think this is exactly why the Bible tells pastors in 2 Timothy 4:2, *"Preach the word! Be ready in season and out of season. Convince, rebuke, exhort, and all longsuffering and teaching."*

Since it is true that young adults are much more likely to walk with God and stay connected to a local church if they are confident in what they believe and if they can base their beliefs on Biblical truth, it is imperative for pastors and other church educational ministry leaders to systematically and carefully teach the Word of God. Our ministries must produce generation after generation who know what they believe and who are willing to stand up for Biblical truth, no matter what they do following high school.

In 2012, professor and researcher, Thomas Bergler wrote *The Juvenilization of American Christianity,* and released a follow-up work, *From Here to Maturity: Overcoming the Juvenilization of American Christianity* in 2014. Bergler's premise is that the church in America has basically become a "youth rally" with popular music and a feel-good sermon on Sunday mornings.[38] He summarized his research by saying, "Youth ministries have been good at getting adolescents to like Jesus and Christianity. But, neither youth ministries nor *juvenilized* churches have been as good at helping people grow out of an adolescent faith into a spiritually mature one." [39]

Most readers know these familiar verses, but take just a moment to read 2 Timothy 3:16-17: *"All Scripture is given by inspiration of God, and is profitable for doctrine, for reproof, for correction, for instruction in righteousness, . that the man of God may be complete, thoroughly equipped for every good work."* It's important to remember that the Bible is not only the inspired Word of God, but It is also "profitable," or beneficial, or practical. In other words, the Bible relates to life[40] in four specific areas: doctrine, reproof, correction, and instruction in righteousness. Notice that the progression here begins with "doctrine"—the systematic teaching of the Scriptures. That word as used here, "does not refer to the process or method of teaching but to its context."[41] This is why it is so important to teach the "whole counsel of God" (see Acts 20:27), so that our young people grow up knowing what they believe and why.

As Cameron Cole, the editor of *Gospel-Centered Youth Ministry* puts it, "While no simple, 'magic bullet' answer exists, I would submit that exegetical Bible teaching may be the wisest practice we can employ in forming kids with lasting faith."[42]

I think there is a negative stereotype that promotes the idea that today's young people do not want truth; that deep teaching of Scripture is not important or that it will not attract teenagers and young adults. This attitude must be destroyed. First of all, it's not Biblical. Second, it's not true. Here's what recent research actually revealed about this generation: "[We were] struck by how the commitment to take Jesus' message seriously is both a demonstrated action and an overall spirit or ethos in [growing] churches."[43]

This does not mean that churches should lecture incessantly or bore our students with Biblical facts or rote, unimaginative lessons. God forbid. Instead, churches must creatively, completely, and carefully present the Scriptures in a way that definitely relates to life today!

2. <u>Help emerging adults get involved and develop "sweat equity" in their local church</u>. This strategy continues with a specific action step to help teenagers and young

adults grow up with a loyalty to their own local church. The key to building "sweat equity" is to help youths realize this is *their* church—to give them a sense of ownership in what the church does. This can be manifested especially through ministry endeavors, physical work projects, connections with other church members, financial giving, and even active participation or voting in church business meetings. All of these things can be tangible and specific ways for your church's young people to build loyalty in the church.

I believe it is a dangerous sign if teenagers demonstrate more of a continuing allegiance to the youth group than they do to the church as a whole. This scenario may be true for a while and may even be somewhat positive as a means to help teens assimilate into the church body. But, let's face it, as young people grow up there will come a time when they graduate from high school and leave the youth group setting. That's why it is important for them to have a connection to the larger church family. So, be sure to remember that the above listed ideas for building loyalty to the church (serving, giving, etc.) should be things the individual teens do in the church as a whole and not just in the youth group. Wise youth workers will supply specific avenues for teenagers and young adults to get actively involved in the big picture of the church program.

3. **Provide ways to promote and demonstrate Godliness from significant, influential adults.** Members of emerging generations desperately need Godly adult models—interested and caring older adults who actively demonstrate and validate what it means to live out the Gospel faithfully over years and years. This kind of ministry is exemplified in passages such as 1 Thessalonians 1:6-7, "*And you became followers of us and of the Lord, having received in word in much affliction, with joy of the Holy Spirit, so that you became examples to all in*

Macedonia and Achaia who believe." And 1 Corinthians 11:1, *"Imitate me, just as I also imitate Christ."* The Bible is packed with illustrations of how important it is for newer believers to have Godly examples they can follow. In both of these passages, the emphasis is on the importance of following and imitating Christ! Of course, our perfect example is the Lord Jesus Christ Himself, but the next generation desperately needs that modeled by influential adults.

We are working with a HDTV and *YouTube* generation. Technology dominates their lives. Yet, we must not forget that the best visual aid ever is not the latest special effects movie; rather, it is the lives of Godly older adults who takes the time and the interest to live out their faithful and genuine relationship with Christ in front of a new generation. That's why I believe it is so important for church leaders to be intentional about connecting significant and Godly adults with young people. In fact, everywhere I go, I encourage youth workers to think about asking senior citizens to serve as youth leaders. Of course, it's possible to get too old to play tackle football, but one never gets too old to minister to kids or to live as an example in front of them.

One of the best things we can do to encourage this to happen is to create opportunities in our regular programming for older saints to tell their story (or "testimony" as my generation would call it) to young people. This could be done as part of a Sunday School class or youth group session, or it could be done in an organized game night or fellowship dinner that is planned specifically for this purpose. Just provide time for the faithful, older people in your church to share a little bit about what it means to live for Christ over the long haul.

4. **Help them build growing inter-generational connections in your church**. Today's children and young people must grow up knowing that God's church is inter-generational. It's time to shatter the outmoded, age-segregated philosophy that has dominated traditional churches for way too long,[44] with the children in one room, the youth in another, the adults in another, and the senior adults somewhere else. I want readers to understand that I am a big fan of peer ministry (e.g., children's ministry, youth ministry, young adult ministry, etc.), but these age-based ministries **must** be balanced with inter-generational connections. The church should be a place where peers gather realizing that God is at work in the lives of people at the same stage of life; but the church must also be a place where kids can connect with older adults who love them and who are committed to welcoming them into the greater body of believers.

Here is a simple chart that illustrates the important balance necessary in churches between "one generational ministries" or peer ministries, like children's ministry, youth ministry, senior citizen's ministry, etc.; "multi-generational ministries," like typical worship services; and "inter-generational ministries," which the various generations intentionally connect with each other.

BALANCED APPROACH TO MINISTRY

ONE-GENERATIONAL MINISTRY

MULTI-GENERATIONAL MINISTRY

INTER-GENERATIONAL MINISTRY

(Additional ideas and details for making inter-generational connections can be found in the Appendix.)

Today's young people certainly need the discipline and instruction[45] of Godly and supportive parents. Kids who have consistent, Godly, and Christ-centered parents certainly have a spiritual advantage. But, the coming generations also need other models and examples. As I mentioned earlier, current cultural trends are indicating that as Christ tarries before His return, more and more young people will be from non-traditional, weak, poor, or dysfunctional family backgrounds. This is the beauty of both the discipleship and mentoring relationships as illustrated and described for us in the Scriptures.

Remember our discussion earlier about John Mark? He grew up as a church kid in a very supportive home. In fact, the early church met in his mother's house.[46] Of course, that was a huge benefit to his long-term spiritual development. But other significant adult mentors certainly played a role in John Mark's growth in Christ. The Apostle Paul, Barnabas, and Peter were all involved in his life, and unquestionably other Godly adults were as well, since the church gathered in his home for their all-night prayer meeting as described in Acts 12:1-19.

John Mark went along with Barnabas and Saul (soon to be renamed Paul) on the First Missionary Journey[47] and then something disastrous happened. Young John Mark abandoned the team and went home.[48] That experience could have meant it was the end of the road in John Mark's spiritual maturation process. But instead Barnabas continued to build into his life, and then he was mentored by Peter[49] (the one person in the Biblical narrative who perhaps more than anyone else knew what it was like to fail and then come back strong[50]).

Obviously, other significant and Godly adults had a major influence in this young man's life.

There is another very important reason why inter-generational relationships are so important for the church—and that is because young people often add life, energy, and enthusiasm to the life of a church.

According to Kara Powell, Jake Mulder, and Brad Griffin in their book *Growing Young: 6 Essential Strategies to Help Youth People Discover and Love Your Church*, "Every church needs young people. Their passion enriches the soil around them. The curiosity they bring to Scripture and the authenticity they bring to relationships keep your church's teaching fresh and fellowship fruitful. Young people also need a thriving church. A thriving church both grounds them in community and sends them out to serve." They aptly conclude, "Your church needs young people, and they your church. One without the other is incomplete."[51]

What Should Christian Parents Do to Keep Emerging Generations From Walking Away?

I am a parent and a grandparent. I can't begin to explain here how important it is to my wife and me that our children and now our grandchildren grow in spiritual maturity. I talk about this quite often and I need to clearly state here, that this fact is totally because of God's grace. But our own three children are now adults, are all living for the Lord, and are serving Him in career ministry. We are now praying daily for our grandchildren to all come to Christ and to live faithfully for Him throughout their lives. The Lord has given me the opportunity to impact thousands of lives of young people over the years, but most important to us is that our own family members live as true believers dedicated to their Lord and Savior Jesus Christ. Humanly speaking, this is the top priority of my life. It is more important to us than if they become great athletes, or if they are wealthy, or even if they are healthy and safe. Most of all, we want our kids and grandkids to grow up to live authentically for the Lord and to serve Him with their lives.

This section of this book then is my practical advice to other parents regarding specific things they can do to help steer their own children toward a life of righteousness. So, I want to go on record right here as saying to other Christian parents, if you feel the same way and if you are willing to do everything you can to help your children grow up and go on for God, then please consider these proactive suggestions.

1. **Make sure your children learn the Scriptures and know how to apply it to their daily lives.** Parents, I urge you for your kids' sake, get them in the Word. Christian parents must follow the example of Timothy's family as pointed out to us in 2 Timothy 3:15, *"from childhood[52] you have known the Holy Scriptures, which are able to make you wise for salvation through faith which is in Christ Jesus."*

   They need to hear from God for a variety of essential reasons:
   - First of all, because they will come to Christ through the Scriptures. Romans 10:17 says, *"So then faith comes by hearing, and hearing by the word of God."*
   - Second, spiritual growth comes from the Word of God. Take a look at 1 Peter 2:2, *"As newborn babes, desire the pure milk of the word, that you may grow thereby."*
   - Next, the Bible keeps them from sin. Psalm 119:11 puts it this way, *"Your word have I hidden in my heart, That I might not sin against You."*
   - The Bible assures us that the Scriptures provide direction for practical life situations. 2 Timothy 2:16-17 says, *"All Scripture is given by inspiration of God, and is profitable for doctrine, for reproof, for correction, for instruction in righteousness, that the man of God may be complete, thoroughly equipped for every good work."*

- It provides wisdom for living, as Colossians 3:16 reminds us, *"Let the word of Christ dwell in you richly in all wisdom."*
- Also, living by the precepts of God's Word brings blessings from God. James 1:22 and 25 tell us, *"But be doers of the word, and not hearers only, deceiving yourselves...he who looks into the perfect law of liberty and continues in it, is not a forgetful hearer but a doer of the work, this one will be blessed in what he does."*

Aren't all of those things what we want for our kids?

I personally remain very, very thankful for the importance my own parents placed on the Word of God. They modeled for us the importance of daily time in God's Word and required us to do the same. They motivated my brothers and me to memorize Scripture passages and helped us apply the corresponding principles to our lives. They taught us to use our Bibles and to search the Scriptures for answers to life's hard questions. They also set the precedent that church and church programs that taught and preached the Bible were to be of high importance in our lives, and didn't allow school, sports, work, or other activities to come before that priority in our schedules.

2. **Build loyalty toward the local church in the lives of your kids.** As I just mentioned, church and church activities were very, very important in our family growing up. My parents (who I'll talk about later in the book) were not in vocational ministry at all. For most of my upbringing, my dad delivered furniture and appliances for Sears; and my mom spent many years working as the night receptionist in the emergency room of our small town hospital. But, they made our local church a top priority for our family. I grew up as the consummate *church kid*. We were involved in everything

the church did—and I really believe it was one of the reasons why my older brother and I grew up to go into career ministry. My parents were consistent about our involvement in church. Nothing was more important in our schedules than that.

Suffice it here for me to say to the Christian parents reading this book, please make church a priority for your young people as well. I have found that if kids think the church isn't important, they'll think God isn't important either. In a young person's mind, the church equals God. Because of that fact, nothing in our family's schedules has more significance and importance attached to it than God's work in the world today—His church! (I will present some specifics about how this can work for parents later on in the book.)

It's amazing for me to think that some parents today will commit to Little League baseball, community soccer leagues, ballet, karate lessons, or to the school band, but they don't commit to something with eternal value.[53] I want to say this to those parents with all sincerity and humility: you are making a big mistake. I really believe that if Christian parents want to invest in something important for their kids that will last for their lifetime, and even for eternity, then get them involved in God's work.

When I was writing to church leaders above, I emphasized the idea that loyalty to the church is built over time by a commitment to ministry endeavors, physical work projects, connections with other church members, financial giving, and active participation in church business. Parents, I highly encourage you to help your children see the importance of the local church by getting them personally and habitually involved in these five specific church-life priorities as well.

3. **Help your children get to know other adults and help them develop healthy and growing relationships with other Godly adults in your church.** This is an important practice I will underscore over and over again in this book. Parents, it is so important to help your children see that there are other Godly adults in the church. They need to get to know multiple authentic examples of adults who are committed to Christ and who have faithfully lived for Him throughout their lives. Children also need to see that there are adults in your church who have lived through some bumps along the way in their lives, but are now living victorious Christian lives.

Like the example of John Mark that I referred to earlier, our children need multiple adult models.[54] That's the basic idea behind the phrase *"multitude of counselors"* in Proverbs 11:14, 15:22, and 24:6. God uses a variety of people—adults who God can speak truth into their lives during their formative years—to impact kids.

I have met some Christian parents in my travels who have the arrogance to believe that they are the only ones who can impact their kids. That is a huge mistake. Our kids need other adult models. I want to reiterate the point that our kids need healthy and growing relationships with other Godly adults. This will help them see how God works in the lives of other people, it will show them that God's work is bigger than their individual family situation, and these relationships will help them transition from children's and youth ministries to the adult ministries in the church.

We'll talk more about how to make these relationships happen later on in the book.

Conversations with Young Adults Who Stayed in the Church: Why They Didn't Walk Away

As I looked into the phenomenon of young adults leaving the church following active involvement in youth group,

I took the opportunity to interview dozens of young adults who have not abandoned their faith and who have not walked away from church.

I purposely spent some time identifying and interviewing Christian young adults who remain active in church to try to pinpoint the common denominators of why they stayed. I am personally very thankful that my ministries have included a great deal of access to a multitude of young adults who are living for the Lord and who are active in His work.

I talked with scores of young adults who are now personally involved in church and I asked them why they didn't walk away. Here's what I found:

1. **Young adults are less likely to drop out of church if their parents demonstrated a genuine love for the Lord.** The majority of young adults I talked to described the consistent Christian testimony of their parents as the most important role model in their lives. If their parents' faith is real, the kids know it, and they are much more likely to want a genuine faith of their own. The conclusion was clear; young adults are much more likely to remain plugged in to church themselves if they grew up in homes where their parents were genuine, Godly role models.

   I did talk with some young adults who are now very active in church, but grew up in non-Christian or incredibly dysfunctional families. These individuals each spoke of a clear message of God's grace that overcame human sinfulness and weaknesses.

   The takeaway here was clear: Christian young adults are much more likely to remain plugged in to church themselves if their parents were genuine, Godly role models. Yes, there were exceptions to that general rule; but in those cases God's grace did something miraculous that overruled the missteps of the parents.

2. **Young adults are less likely to drop out of church if their parents were consistent about their own personal and family commitment to the local church.** Again, the majority of these young adults talked about the commitment their parents had made to the church during their own formative years. Several shared anecdotes of parents who "never missed a service" or who "made us go to Sunday School and youth group." Some spoke about not being allowed to take jobs or get involved in sports or other extra-curricular activities if that interfered with church functions. It was clear, if the parents made church a priority, the kids most often grew up making church a priority too.

3. **Young adults are less likely to drop out of church if they have experienced the church working in collaboration with their parents for the spiritual growth of the young person.** Every one of the young adults I interviewed spoke highly of a significant adult, often several adults, who took a personal interest in them during their days growing up in church. My own personal interest in youth ministry was stirred when I heard so many speak about the youth pastors or lay youth workers who played an active role in their lives. They each identified various Godly adults who cared enough to build a personal relationship with them during their maturing years. My conclusion following these conversations was obvious—the positive relationships they had with Godly adults was a key factor in their long term spiritual growth.

4. **Young adults are less likely to drop out of church if they have been actively involved in specific ministry and service initiatives throughout their lives as children and teenagers.** Another conclusion was also clear—if the church only focused on entertaining kids and not involving them in the greater life of the church, once they became adults they would most likely walk

away. The converse is also true—if the church (and youth ministry) was intentional and missional about involving young people in specific ministry and service projects, the participants were more likely to stay involved in those things into adulthood.

Again, the takeaway here was clear: youth programs don't work—youth *ministry* does work, and it lasts!

5. **<u>Young adults are less likely to drop out of church if they see the relevance and importance of Biblical truth and can vividly see how God's Word applies to their current lives.</u>** My final observation seemed to jump out of every single conversation. Young adults who see God's Word as relevant and related to their lives are the ones who also see the church as vitally important. They realize that the Church has been designed by God to help people come to Christ and grow in Him into spiritual maturity. These young adults participate in church to worship Him and to hear God's Word taught.

I absolutely loved talking to these young adults. They each craved the opportunity to be a part of an inter-generational community of Christ-followers who gathered together often to open the Scriptures together because they knew they needed to grow closer to Him.

Now let's continue the conversation about why God's church is so important for families.

"…You must continue in the things which you have learned and been assured of knowing from whom you have learned them."
2 Timothy 3:14

"My manner of life from my youth, which was spent from the beginning among my own nation at Jerusalem, all the Jews know."
Acts 26:4

Conversation #4
Mission-Imperative: What do Christian Parents and Families Need From the Church?
(Or Why Is the Church So Important?)

Do you know *these* kids?

They grew up in a very religious and God-centered environment that included a consistent family influence and a larger community of Godly adults and peers. It was in this atmosphere that they learned the Scriptures—including the importance of living by the Ten Commandments and other Biblical precepts. They grew up understanding the value of true friends and built Godly peers into their lives. They undoubtedly were taught the importance of forming Biblical convictions, which included standing firm on what they were taught, no matter what. And they learned to stand together with other young people who were willing to take a stand for the truth as well.

As these young men grew up, their peaceful and idyllic upbringing was shattered by the captivating influence of a negative, evil, and completely different system of religious thought that denied the existence of the One True God. These young men, once sheltered by their families and the spiritual community around them, moved a long way away from home, and were forced to make up their minds very quickly about their own personal beliefs. This new culture around them was increasingly negative and oppressive. This philosophy demanded total allegiance to prideful, powerful leaders and their secular world view.

A confrontation ensued. The young men were faced with a life-threatening dilemma. They could stand up for the faith they held since childhood, or they could give in to the malicious and violent enemy. These young adult believers literally faced a life and death situation simply because of their religious convictions. If they stood up for God they would be killed. If they gave in and acted like everyone else they would live.

This is not the story of contemporary believers in a Communist or Muslim country. Nor did it happen at a large American university. This account is also from the Bible. By now you know that it is taken from Daniel 3; and it is the story of Shadrach, Meshach, and Abednego, three Hebrew young men who were taken captive by the evil leader of Babylon, King Nebuchadnezzar. Babylon was Israel's arch enemy in many ways, including politically, philosophically, and religiously.

The Babylonian ruler rejected Jehovah in favor of worshiping an idol that he set up in an open field near their capital city. A directive was communicated for the people, including the captive slaves from Israel, to gather; and upon the King's command, a band would play, and the people were told to "fall down"[55] in worship before the idol, representing the evil King Nebuchadnezzar.

In most Eastern cultures, the action of bowing down before someone was not just a decree to fall on one's knees. Instead it was an order, of life and death significance here, to fall prostrate,[56] face down on the ground as an act of total surrender to the King. This was the Old Testament meaning of the concept to bow down. It wasn't that Shadrach, Meshach, and Abednego were told to get on their knees. They were commanded to totally lie down, face first in the dirt.

But, they didn't bow down!

It's no wonder the three Hebrew young men were noticed by the Babylonians as they stood tall in the midst of the throng of people who were actually lying on the ground. The proud Nebuchadnezzar was furious, so he commanded his soldiers to bring the insubordinate men before his throne. His command was for total allegiance. It was literally a mandate to worship him and that presented Shadrach, Meshach, and Abednego with a huge dilemma. If they bowed down, it would violate the Biblical convictions they had learned and practiced since childhood. These young men understood the Ten Commandments and they knew what God meant in Exodus 20:3-6:

> You shall have no other gods before Me. You shall not make for yourself a carved image—any likeness of anything that is in heaven above, or that is in the earth beneath, or that is in the water under the earth; you shall not bow down to them nor serve them. For I, the Lord your God, am a jealous God, visiting the iniquity of the fathers upon the children to the third and fourth generations of those who hate Me, but showing mercy to thousands, to those who love Me and keep My commandments.

The three young Hebrews weren't going to worship an idol of an enemy king—no matter what the ramifications were; and that meant that they were sentenced to die a gruesome, fiery death.

But they didn't lie down. They kept their convictions and stood for their beliefs no matter what everyone else did. Their faith was real, and they believed (they knew!) that the Almighty God could protect them. They also knew it was a very real possibility for them to suffer and even die for standing for their convictions. Yet they kept standing.

King Nebuchadnezzar was incensed. He was livid. So he ordered Shadrach, Meshach, and Abednego to die in a "burning fiery furnace."

You know the rest of the story. God intervened and kept His followers safe from the inconceivable and unimaginable heat of the furnace. Nebuchadnezzar was absolutely "astonished"[57] and commanded his soldiers to bring the Hebrew young adults out of the fire. God blessed them for standing up for their convictions. God kept them safe and used Shadrach, Meshach, and Abednego to change the course of history.

The lessons here are obvious. They kept their convictions, regardless of what happened to them, and God blessed. I love the fact that these three young men are always mentioned together in the Biblical text. There's something quite powerful about growing up in a community of faith and knowing there are others who have the same beliefs and same convictions.

Isn't that what we want for our kids today? We want them to grow up with a genuine and personal faith, have the courage to stand up for their convictions, and stand with others who believe the same things?

Raising *Our* Kids Today in a Community of Faith– *Inter-Generational Family Ministry*

God never intended for parents to raise their kids in a vacuum away from other Godly and important influences in their lives. Both parents and children need the positive and caring encouragement that comes from growing up and living in a community with other dedicated Christ-followers. As one blog post from the "Sticky Faith" team at Fuller Youth Institute puts it, "Throughout Scripture, God paints a picture of kids being raised by parents working hand in hand with the broader adult community."[58] This is exactly why this book is advocating what I am calling "inter-generational *family* ministry." Christian parents must see the need to raise their children as an active part of a community of faith that (1) includes the encouraging impact of other Godly adults upon the lives of the next generation[59] **AND** (2) that embraces the importance of building Godly peers as positive influences into the lives of our kids.

This philosophy was modeled throughout the Old Testament in passages like Deuteronomy 6:1-25. Notice this familiar text, that is so often directed at parents only, begins with the phrase, *"Hear, O Israel"* in both verses 3 and 4. Plus, it's an important observation to note the passage's use of the pronouns, *"you"* and *"your"* are used in a plural sense throughout the text. Also, Deuteronomy begins with, *"These are the words which Moses spoke to all Israel"*; and that the phrase *"all Israel"* is mentioned at least 12 times throughout the book. It's quite obvious that the familiar instructions of the *Shema* passage in Deuteronomy 6 were intended for the entire community. In other words, even in the Old Testament Jewish culture, being a part of a faith community was essential for raising children.

This is why the local church is so important for young people today—our kids desperately need an inter-generational community of faith that includes growing and encouraging relationships with Godly adults; they need friendships with peers who can stand with them in an increasingly hostile and secular culture. That is exactly the kind of environment where Shadrach, Meshach, and Abednego grew up. They were taught the Scriptures in a strong and consistent community that also produced peers who could stand for God together.

Of course the church also exists to provide a setting for "worship, fellowship, discipleship, ministry, and evangelism" (we'll talk more about these "purposes" in Conversation #5), which are all critical aspects of the "Purpose-Driven Church," as identified by popular pastor, Rick Warren.[60] Although Warren is the one most credited for giving credence to these five *purposes*, it is nonetheless true that only a faith community—a local church—can truly provide a setting for these functions to take place. Yes, Godly parents can fulfill some of the duties associated with "worship, fellowship, discipleship, ministry, and evangelism." In a family setting, for instance, parents can intentionally provide Christian *fellowship* for their kids, and can involve their children in various forms of ministry and *evangelism*. But Biblically speaking, these functions are to be aspects of a local church. (See list below.)

Wise Christian parents will make sure their kids grow up in a faith community because there are unquestionably several key Biblical mandates for believers that can only be provided in and through a local body of believers[61] living in inter-generational community with each other. These directives for Christ-followers include:

- Discipleship – Matthew 28:19 -20; 2 Timothy 2:2
- Mentoring – 1 Thessalonians 2:8; Titus 2:1-10
- Preaching – 1 Timothy 4:2; Acts 20:28
- Teaching – Ephesians 4:11; 1 Timothy 5:17; James 1:22
- Ministry or service – Ephesians 4:12; 2 Timothy 2:16-18
- Fellowship & community – 1 Corinthians 12:21-26; Hebrews 10:25
- Care – 1 Corinthians 12:12-21; 1 Timothy 5:3-16
- Evangelism & outreach – Acts 1:8; 1 Timothy 4:5; 1 Peter 3:15
- Worship through music – Ephesians 5:19; Colossians 3:17
- Giving – 1 Corinthians 16:1-2; 2 Corinthians 8:1-5; 2 Corinthians 9:6-7: Philippians 4:10-20
- Pastoral influence & authority – Acts 20:28; Ephesians 4:11, 1 & 2 Timothy and Titus; 1 Peter 5:1-4
- Spiritual accountability – 1 Timothy 5:3-16; Hebrews 13:7; 1 Peter 5:5

The New Testament is full of specific action items for believers that can only truly be accomplished via a local church. As we'll talk about later on in the book, this does not mean that any individual local church is perfect. Even the specific local churches that are mentioned or referred to in Scripture are listed with both strengths and weaknesses. But the point remains that our kids need the church. This is what Christ intended, and it is imperative for parents to understand that kids need that community environment as they grow and develop. God never intended growth toward spiritual maturity to happen in a vacuum or even within individual family units alone. As one writer put it, "As much as faith in Jesus is about a 'personal relationship,' it can only be worked out in community."[62] The New Testament pattern was for genuine, long-term growth to happen within the confines of community. It is in the church where our kids will find mentors and it is in the church where they will find good friends.

Why Christian Parents Should Make Church Youth Ministry a Priority

It's important for parents to realize that involvement in church is essential. It's too easy in today's culture to look at church youth ministry as just one other option for their kids. One youth ministry blogger put it this way, "Students along with their parents see fellowship, gathered worship, church, and youth group as electives. Our post-modern, determine-your-own-values-and-reality mindset has finally trickled its way into the local church." He continues, "Now church, youth group, and actually any spiritual discipline are firmly on the bottom of the pecking order. This means that if homework, sports, vacation, being tired, practice, fill in the blank, don't conflict then both students and their parents might consider attending some gathered Christian event like church or youth group."[63]

One reason attending church is important for your children is because this is a place where they are likely to forge important Christian relationships. Parents should remember one key element of the story of Shadrach, Meshach, and Abednego and that is this: the three Hebrew young men are always mentioned together. I briefly mentioned this then, but let's revisit the importance of it here. I believe it was much easier for Shadrach to stand for God because the others stood also, and the same could be said of the other two as well. The text never says that explicitly, but in the situation in Daniel 3, when the others were on their faces in the dirt, Shadrach, Meshach, and Abednego stood tall for their convictions **together**. I often preach a message emphasizing this principle in Daniel 3 when I speak to teenagers. I want them to see the value of having good friends— friends with the spiritual depth and maturity to stand for what they believe no matter what.

Parents, church youth groups are the place where your children are likely to find other young people like that.

There are certainly very valid reasons for having a strong and effective church youth ministry.[64] It's not time to overreact and eliminate the many positive aspects of youth ministry in favor of all ages meeting together for one more lecture in the church auditorium.[65] I believe that the key is balance. I am convinced that today's churches can and should balance their programming and methods so that peer ministry can exist and thrive alongside inter-generational connections.

Why Other Godly Adults Are So Important for Young People

Dr. Chap Clark, well-known youth ministry professor, writer, and researcher, has made the assertion that today's teenagers need strong relationships with five significant adults (other than their parents) if they are going to continue involvement in church following their youth ministry years.[66] He wrote, "Here's the bottom line: every kid needs five adult fans. Any young person who shows any interest in Christ needs a minimum of five people of various ages who will say, 'I'm going to love that kid until they are fully walking as an adult member of this congregation.'"[67]

Our young people need Godly adults to be actively involved in their lives. I believe it is essential for the spiritual development of youth that older, Godly adults take the initiative to build growing relationships with them. This is a key reason why the local church is so important for Christian families.

So how can churches be proactive and intentionally build five significant, Godly adults into the lives of the next generation? Here are some suggestions:

1. <u>Hire a qualified, trained, and experienced pastor to shepherd your church's youth</u>. I admit it, I am a fan of vocational youth pastors. I've spent the majority of my life involved in local church youth ministry, so I believe in the role of youth pastors. Plus, as a dad, I can't tell you how thankful I am for the ministry youth pastors had in the lives of my kids. According to my friend Wayne Morgan with the *National Network of Youth Ministry*, the majority of young adults who stay in church after they

graduate from high school had a youth pastor who invested in their life.

Let me take a moment to explain the adjectives I used in this sub-point:

- **Qualified**: Pastors, even young youth pastors, must meet the Biblical qualifications found in 1 Timothy 3 and Titus 1, and should fulfill pastoral duties in the church. This could include teaching or preaching God's Word, shepherding and caring, administration and leadership.
- **Trained**: Youth pastors should be trained before they begin. Of course, this training could include a Bible College or Seminary education, and perhaps a church-based internship or apprenticeship ministry. (In fact, if your church is looking for a youth pastor, the placement, career services, or alumni departments of trusted colleges and seminaries would be a great place to start the search.) Youth pastors should know what they are talking about and they need to know what they are doing. And, are they called of God to do this?
- **Experienced**: As a parent or church leader, I don't want someone we pay to minister to kids that has never done this before. If someone is really called to be a youth pastor they will already have experience working with teenagers. This experience can be gained in a variety of ways during their days of preparation for the youth pastorate.

2. <u>Recruit a team of Godly, caring adults to serve as lay youth workers in your church</u>. With or without a paid youth pastor, your church needs a team of Godly and caring adults to work with teenagers. Please notice the plurality of my terms. I believe in team ministry—a variety of adult models who can reach and minister to a variety of teens. In other words, some singles and some married couples, some younger adults, and some older

adults, and so on. Be sure to include a variety of ages, ethnicities, and geographical backgrounds on the team. The main responsibility of any lay youth worker must be to build growing relationships with teens. That really is the key. Genuine opportunities to teach and disciple will develop from growing, positive relationships.

3. <u>Recruit and train competent adults to minister as small group leaders in your youth group</u>. Your small group leaders are another level of adult interaction with students. Be sure to identify and then recruit adults who have the ability to guide discussions around the Scriptures, and who can think on their feet in case the teens ask challenging questions, or want to talk about difficult life situations. I think it's also wise to look for small group leaders who are able and willing to interact with the students on occasions outside of small group. (Some churches are organizing their entire small group ministry around inter-generational connections; and of course, this would add an interesting dynamic to this type of ministry structure.)

4. <u>Identify interested, Godly adults to intentionally mentor young people</u>. Titus 2 has been labeled by some as the most powerful and practical passage in Scripture on the idea of church-based mentoring. (Much more about the concept of mentoring will be presented in Conversation #7.) Even in the 1st century, the Apostle Paul told Titus that he'd have to teach the people to interact with other generations. Perhaps, there has always been a generation gap (even there in 1st century Crete), yet Paul wrote this set of instructions to remind them about the importance of older people ministering to younger people in the church. It's the same today. Pastors and other church leaders will need to look for ways to motivate older believers to reach out to younger people. Notice the practicality in Titus 2. This passage screams real-life

situations—and that's the beauty of mentoring. It's doing what you do—just doing it with someone younger.

5. <u>Utilize other significant adults to serve your youth group</u>. Another way to build adults into the lives of the young people in your church is to use significant Godly adults in various ways within your existing youth ministry. Here are some practical ideas to consider:
   - Recruit parents of teenagers or other adults to accompany your group on youth events or trips.
   - Invite church leaders to speak, teach, or otherwise participate in youth group meetings.
   - Ask the lead pastor or other pastoral staff members to teach on a specific topic in youth group.
   - Involve some Godly adults who have unique life experiences to minister to students who are facing some of the same experiences.
   - Give older, Godly adults the opportunity to share their story (or their testimony) with teenagers.
   - Schedule opportunities for other inter-generational social and ministry connections in your church.

   (Of course, you'll need to be cognizant of your church's policy on child protection or use of potential background checks before making these decisions.)

6. <u>Identify some Godly parents of teenagers to build healthy, growing relationships with their kids' friends</u>. Parents of kids in your church can be some of the most ideal people to minister to their kids' friends, especially if you have young people involved in your ministry who are from dysfunctional home situations. When our own children were teenagers, we often encouraged them to invite their friends over to our house. This provided a safe atmosphere for our kids and gave us the opportunity to get to know their friends. Even now that

our kids are grown, my wife and I still have close relationships with some of their friends from youth groups days.

7. <u>Motivate your church's senior citizens to pray specifically and intentionally for young people—by name</u>! I am excited about a growing trend around the country to intentionally involve senior citizens in specific ways with teenagers and young adults. Your church's older adults have much more to offer than simply listening to the memory verses in the children's club program. For example, I am doing everything I can to encourage churches to include senior citizens as part of their team of volunteer youth workers. It's sad to think that many of our churches' oldest members feel like they are being put out to pasture, when they have actually accumulated years-and-years-and-years of incredible ministry skills to impact generation after generation of young people in the church.

Involving senior citizens in a significant way absolutely needs to start with prayer. Do whatever you can to motivate your church's oldest adults to pray specifically, by name for the young people. I visited one church that printed baseball card-sized photographs with biographical sketches on the back of each teen in the youth group and distributed them to the senior citizen's Sunday School class for prayer. Other churches simply circulated a list of names and grades that gave the seniors enough information for them to pray intelligently for the teens. This practice will put a growing burden on their hearts for the students; and it has the potential to revolutionize your church and help shatter its generation gap!

I am convinced that by implementing some of the ideas listed above, your church can build that five-adults-to-one-student ratio that is so essential to help our young people grow up and go on for God.

Making This Personal

I have made the case fairly emphatically that Christian parents should make a commitment to involve their kids in church. So many parents are willing to have their children commit to temporal things in life instead of things that matter for eternity.

To lead our children, my wife and I tried to make some conscious choices for what we wanted for our family. In other words, we developed a philosophical grid through which we made decisions for what our kids would do or would not do.

Here is a simple illustration that may help readers understand this point. I grew up in a small town in Northeastern Pennsylvania. Our town was so small that we had one street light, one bank, one small movie theater, two family restaurants, and two rather small grocery stores. On occasion, my father would have our entire family walk to "the store," which meant we would walk the few blocks to the closest grocery store. So one summer evening my Dad, Mom, my older brother, my younger brother, and I started our walk to the local Acme Store. Somewhere along the route, my younger brother found a white canvas bag with black lettering on the side, and a metal clasp on the top. As young boys are prone to do, he started playing make-believe football with the bag. He threw imaginary touchdowns to himself, kicked make-believe field goals, and even spiked the bag in made-up end zones. After a few blocks my Dad noticed the bag and realized that the black lettering on the side of the canvas bag was actually the name of the bank in our town. Come to find out, the bag was filled with money—an assortment of small bills of various denominations, and a deposit slip from the Acme Store. We found out later that the manager placed the bag of money on top of his car on the way to make the deposit at the bank and then drove off. Somewhere on his journey, the bag fell off the top of his car and my little brother then made his discovery of the bag, which became his imaginary football.

My parents realized this could become a teachable moment for their sons; so of course, we took the bag back to the store. I remember my little brother standing inside the grocery store near the manager's office waiting to get the manager's attention. We could almost see the wheels of memory and shock turning in his head when he realized this little boy had found the bag of money and had returned it to the store. He had totally forgotten that he never even made the deposit.

In exchange for my brother's show of honesty in returning the money bag, the manager decided to reward my brother with a quick shopping spree in the store. He let my brother take a shopping cart and gave him a brief time limit, letting him know that he could take anything he wanted from the store—all he had to do was get back to the manager's office before the time limit. "Ready, set, go." And my brother was off like a shot—returning long before the time was up with his grocery cart filled with... candy! He had selected one kind of hard candy and put several bags of it into his cart. If memory serves me correctly, our mother began to cry and seemed to mutter the word "meat" over and over again under her breath.

In many ways, our lives are like that simple story from my childhood. It's as if God gives us a life-sized grocery cart and the freedom to go aisle to aisle making choices of what we put into our carts. Family life is often like that. Parents can make a series of choices for their children—we can make wise, lasting choices, or impulsive, short-term choices. Raising children is much more important than selecting hard candy—it involves making God-honoring choices that will impact them for the rest of their lives and into eternity as they grow up making their own spiritually-oriented decisions.

Here then is the basic philosophy my wife Peggy and I used in raising our children:

1. From the day each of our three children were born, we prayed that they would come to Christ and live their lives for Him.
2. We wanted them to learn and understand the Bible— and then grow up making their own decisions based upon Biblical principles.

3. The local church is God's work in the world. It is important and we wanted them to enjoy their involvement in church functions.
4. Serving the Lord is a great privilege, so we worked hard to find ways our family could serve Him together as well as individually.

Before listing and explaining the practical choices we made for our children based upon this simple parenting philosophy, I need to provide a bit of autobiographical information. I served as a youth pastor when our children were born; but when they were young, God directed us into another ministry direction that included opportunities for me to serve the Lord in two different Christian colleges, at a denominational publishing company, and as a leader of a non-profit, religious organization. I want readers to know our family's background to say this: I haven't served in the pastorate for many, many years. Even though we served in a variety of vocational ministry positions, in many ways we served the Lord as *lay* people in the two different churches we have attended since our days in local church ministry. So, the choices I am about to describe are not the decisions of a pastor's family. The choices we made for our family were intentional based upon the philosophical filters listed above.

Also, in many ways, ours was a typical American family, with very busy family and personal schedules. This included a great deal of ministry travel, a full calendar of school functions, including homework, extra-curricular activities like Little League baseball and community basketball leagues, jobs for our kids to save money for college, plus their involvement in many of the programs planned for various ministries at the church. So, we made the following church functions as key priorities for our children and built these six choices into our family's regular calendar.

1. God's Word – We wanted our children to love and appreciate the teaching and preaching of the Bible. So ministries that featured the exposition of Scripture and creative Bible teaching were central for our family. For

example, even when our kids were young children (beyond their days in the church nursery), we had them sit with us during the church services and encouraged them to take notes. Now that all three of our children are grown up, they each still take notes during sermons, and they each are actively involved in individual ministries where the presentation of Scripture is a key aspect of what they do.

2. <u>Worship</u> – We understood that the use of music in worship was also very important for our kids. My wife and I came to the understanding very early in our lives as parents that our kids' tastes in music were quite different than ours, and we came to the conclusion that we were okay with that. We believed that it was important for them to have a musical expression for true worship, and that worship ministries were very important for their generation. Our feeling was that if their musical choices did not violate a clear principle in Scripture, then their individual taste in music was fine with us.

3. <u>Service</u> – We definitely saw serving the Lord as a key ingredient for living for Christ. Even though I no longer served in the pastorate, we wanted ministry to be a major focus of their lives. For several years now, Peggy and I have looked for ways we can serve the Lord together in and through our local church. Over the years, we have spent the vast majority of our time serving in various aspects of youth ministry and now in young adult ministry. We wanted our kids to see that we loved serving Him and that a true outflow of our Christian lives was a commitment to doing whatever we could to serve Him, especially in ways that allowed us to use our gifts, talents, abilities, and experience to make an impact for eternity.

4. <u>Fellowship</u> – We realized how important friends are to teenagers, and we also knew that peer pressure is an incredibly powerful influence on them. I heard a well-known youth ministry specialist several years ago say, "Friends are the lifeblood of adolescents." So we were determined to make sure that our kids found good friends in and through our churches' youth ministries and various other youth ministry events that were a part of what we did as a family. For example, I have often joked that our kids have visited every Christian camp in the country because they usually went with me when I traveled to camps as a youth speaker. Plus, we encouraged them to participate in local, regional, national, and even international youth meetings, rallies, conferences, and events so that they would see that there are tons of other Christian young people out there who love the Lord and who are attempting to stand for Him. We wanted them to experience the "Shadrach, Meshach, and Abednego factor" I talked about earlier in this chapter of how these three young Hebrew men are always mentioned together. That is a vivid example of the importance of good friends in the lives of young people. When our kids were teenagers, they never wanted us to go away from home very long because they hated to miss youth group—their friends were there.

5. <u>Giving</u> – We knew that giving and generosity are also important virtues, so we encouraged each of them to be generous as soon as they were at the age where they were earning some money. We wanted them to understand the Biblical concept of "stewardship" and that everything we have belongs to God, not us. As I have mentioned several times in this book, our three children are now all in career ministry as adults—and in one way or another, all three receive their life's income from ministry. Learning the value of trusting

God and giving to Him and to others is something they learned early in life.

6. <u>Evangelism</u> – We also wanted our kids to be serious about sharing their faith with others. Full disclosure is important here: we sent our children to public schools. We certainly understand that it is the parents' responsibility to educate their children—not the Christian school and certainly not the government. We understood the issues involved in that decision, and we did all we could to be involved in our kids' schooling. We went to the parents' meetings, their activities, and often just showed up at their schools. We wanted their teachers and administrators to know we cared about their education and that we were going to be active in the process. But, we also wanted our children to learn how to share the Gospel with others and to be a good witness for Him. I believe that one of the reasons two of our children are now missionaries and the other is actively and purposefully involved in evangelism is because they learned as kids how important outreach really is.

Please understand that the last section is not written in pride or in a veiled attempt to brag about our skills as parents. That is not it at all! I only wanted to add a real-life illustration to the principles and suggestions that were presented in this Conversation. I trust that intent came through in the paragraphs and principles above.

What choices are you putting in to your family's *grocery cart*?

"He who loves father or mother more than Me is not worthy of Me.
And he who loves son or daughter more than Me is not worthy of Me.
And he who does not take his cross and follow after Me
is not worthy of Me." Matthew 10:37-38

Conversation #5
Danger Sign: Has the Family Become More Important Than the Church?

What I am presenting in this chapter may seem somewhat controversial. But I am afraid that the family has become an idol in some Christian environments today. In fact, author and pastor, Kevin DeYoung agrees, and recently made this bold and convicting statement: "One of the acceptable idolatries among evangelical Christians is the idolatry of the family."[68]

Another author, secular columnist John Rosemond, in *Your Kids Should Not Be the Most Important*, adds, "Many if not most of the problems [parents are] having with their kids are the result of treating their children as if they, their marriage, and their family exist because of the kids."[69] Although coming from a different starting point, his point is nonetheless valid. If our kids or our families become more important than what God intended, we have a problem on our hands.

I understand the seriousness of what I am saying. An idol is anything we honor or emphasize more than God or God's plans. It seems to me that many Christian parents are putting their family interests and concerns ahead of the big picture of God's work in the world. I concur with well-known speaker and writer Francis Chan's observation that many Christian parents are choosing to focus on what their own children and families are doing instead of motivating them toward "the mission of God."[70]

We must never forget that God ordained two institutions to help his people grow towards spiritual maturity—the home AND the church. We shouldn't make one of them a priority over the other. And yet that is what is happening when we make our families more important than the church. Many parents today are choosing to put their children's activities and desires ahead of a commitment to the church. We must remember that both institutions are designed by God and are vitally important, for our kids and for us. Practically speaking, Christian parents and church leaders must be absolutely committed to God's purpose for the next generation and that is for them to grow up and go on for God. But that won't happen without the local church.

Too many Christian parents are putting sports, lessons, work, homework, or other seemingly constructive things ahead of a faithful, committed involvement in the church. I believe that Christian parents are making a mistake if they commit to soccer, football, or baseball for their kids instead of making church a top priority for them.

But please hear me out. Recently I had the opportunity to lead interactive discussion times with a wide variety of youth pastors and lay youth workers who represented a national audience of local churches.[71] Our conversation dealt with the common struggles they were facing working with teens and their families. It saddens me to report that these youth pastors collectively indicated that parents' lack of commitment to the church was their main concern. They shared a variety of stories of how Christian parents wanted their kids to be involved in community soccer leagues or some other extracurricular activity. They shared specific illustrations of parents who would commit the resources of time, energy, and money for their kids to be involved in those things, and then demonstrate very little commitment to children's or youth activities at church.

I understand the feelings on both sides of this issue. I was a high school and college athlete, and I can appreciate the commitment it takes to be successful in the world of competitive sports. I am also a parent and a grandparent, and I get it that we want our kids to be successful and popular in those arenas (no pun intended), but I would much rather select activities and involvements for my kids that have eternal value for them

Parental Choices

From my travels, ministries, and conversations with church leaders and parents, I have observed that there are three basic reasons why Christian parents would choose to have their young people involved in activities other than the church.

The first is if parents allow their kids to make the decisions. I have met countless parents who give in to their children's whims and impulses about various involvements. If the kids want to play Little League baseball, they take them to the games. If they want to play the guitar, they provide lessons; and so on. These parents schedule their lives based around the often-fleeting desires of kids. Church functions then take a back seat on the family's priority list.

To be fair, I have also met some committed Christian young people and their parents who make the choice to be involved in sports or other activities because of the child's talent or skill level, and because they can use athletics, for instance, as a platform for sharing Christ. I can understand this motivation and certainly applaud high-level athletes or other performers who use their skills as a matter of stewardship before the Lord.[72]

A second reason why Christian parents might choose extra-curricular activities over church is because of their own personal motivations. Some parents want their kids to be popular within the community or peer group. Other parents are trying to live out their own unfulfilled fantasies in the lives of their children. Others simply want their offspring to be involved in positive and constructive efforts instead of other harmful or negative options. That makes sense, but these functions should never replace the many positive benefits of local church involvements.

The third reason for some parents is that they might be disheartened with church programming and scheduling. It seems as if so many churches became very traditional and quite similar during my generation. The typical Sunday service schedule became predictable and patterned. The day started with age-segregated Sunday School classes followed by a morning worship service, with a set and publicized order of service—hymns, announcements, offering, Scripture reading, another hymn, special music, and then the message. Sundays also included a wide array of meetings, programs, and an evening worship service, with the same basic format as the morning service.

Today's emerging generations are not wired for that kind of schedule. Instead, they crave life-related teaching and life-on-life relationships.

Notice what David Kinnaman, the president of Barna Group and the author of *You Lost Me: Why Young Christians Are Leaving Church...and Rethinking Faith,* has to say: "We are at a critical point in the life of the North American church; the Christian community must rethink our efforts to make disciples. Many of the assumptions on which we have built our work with young people are rooted in modern, mechanistic, and mass production paradigms. Some (though not all) ministries have taken cue from the assembly line, doing everything possible to streamline the manufacture of shiny new Jesus-followers, fresh from the factory floor."[73]

I mentioned earlier the conversations I had with a national group of church youth pastors and youth workers. They were all quite frustrated and somewhat angry with today's parents who choose to put cultural activities for their kids ahead of church programing, including youth group meetings and other youth ministry activities. But I wonder...

Maybe these parents just do not like that cookie-cutter, over-scheduled model of church life. Maybe the church should be more intentional about equipping people for real-life situations. Maybe the church needs to shut down its "assembly line" approach and instead develop a specific, planned approach for authentic, life-related discipleship.[74] Maybe then we'd help today's Christian parents make the important decisions they need to make to raise their kids towards spiritual maturity. This tension boils down to one basic principle: we must be intentional about the choices we make to help young people go on for God.

As I mentioned at the end of Conversation #1, I have often told audiences when I speak on this subject that I would much rather have my children grow up to be Godly than successful. In my heart, I really didn't care if my children grew up to be poor; I care desperately that they are Godly.

It is my opinion that Christian parents are making a bad trade by involving, sometimes even over-involving, their children in community sports or other seemingly wholesome activities to the detriment of their involvement in church.[75]

I really do understand the tension of wanting our children to be involved in community or school activities and the resulting advantages that can come from those involvements. Athletics and other extra-curricular activities can certainly teach kids very positive values like teamwork, effort, discipline, and endurance. But my point here, as a long-time youth worker and parent, is that the lasting spiritual benefit of involvement in church is more important for our kids. It is in church where our kids will learn about worship, discipleship, fellowship, evangelism, and ministry.[76] It is in church where they'll connect with older, Godly mentors, as well as develop lasting friendships with other Christian students. Plus, we must remember that the church is God's plan. It is His idea that the church serves as the conduit for spiritual growth.[77]

Let's identify some important Biblical principles that we may be able to apply to this modern-day situation for today's Christian parents, and then we'll look at a few practical suggestions for both church leaders and parents.

Some Biblical Principles to Consider

There seems to be an incompatibility between the emphasis many church leaders today place upon the traditional "nuclear family"[78] than what is actually taught in Scripture. I certainly appreciate passages such as Deuteronomy 6:1-9, 11:18-21, Psalms 78:1-8, Proverbs 1:8, 22:6, Ephesians 6:1-4, and Colossians 3:20-21, and view the basic teaching of these passages as vitally important for my life and for my family. I understand that parents, especially fathers (as in Ephesians 6:1-4), are to be the primary influencers over their children.[79] I take that responsibility very personally in my own family and I realize that my task as a Christian parent is to point our children toward God and His work for eternity.

However, there are significant Biblical and cultural difficulties with the view that the church exists for strong families only—those families where a father is present and where he is the spiritual head of the family. That is the certainly the preferred situation, and that is the model most presented in Scripture (see Ephesians 5:22-33, combined with 6:1-4.) But there are three basic difficulties with that perspective: (1) Not everyone is from a strong, stable, and spiritually-mature family—for example, Timothy in Acts 16:1; (2) The church is to be a "family" to those who are disenfranchised—see James 1:27; and (3) As time goes on, more and more families will be from non-traditional and dysfunctional families—see 2 Timothy 3:1-9.

Actually, the Bible teaches that family relationships are likely to be obstacles for true followers of Jesus Christ. Take a hard look at the following verses:

Matthew 10:37 *"He who loves father or mother more than Me is not worthy of Me. And he who loves son or daughter more than Me is not worthy of Me."*

Matthew 19:29 *"And everyone who has left houses or brothers or sisters or father or mother or wife or children or lands, for My name's sake, shall receive a hundredfold, and inherit eternal life."*

Luke 14:26-27 *"If anyone comes to Me and does not hate his father and mother, wife and children, brothers and sisters, yes, and his own life also, he cannot be My disciple. And whoever does not bear his cross and come after Me cannot be My disciple."*

Dr. John MacArthur makes this convicting statement in his commentary on Matthew: "A hallmark of discipleship is willingness to forsake everything, including one's own family if necessary, for Christ's sake." He adds, "The Christian is to love his family with self-sacrificing love. Christian husbands and wives are to love each other and their children with unreserved devotion. Christian children are to love, respect, and care for their parents as unto the Lord. But a believer's commitment to Christ is so profound and far-reaching that any relationship that endangers that relationship must be sacrificed if necessary."[80]

Readers, to be honest with you, the trend I have observed seems to be the opposite of that. I know this may sound harsh, but I've met so many parents who appear to sacrifice their children's involvement and participation in God's work for the sake of their relationships with their family members. As I said above, I think that's a bad trade. Our commitment to Christ and to His work must take precedent over everything else.

MacArthur also commented on what Christ exclaimed in Luke 14:26, "The Lord's teaching that it is necessary to hate one's family in not inconsistent with the Bible's commands that children are to honor their parents (Exodus 20:12), husbands love their wives (Ephesians 5:25), wives love their husbands (Titus 2:4), and parents love their children (Titus 2:4; cf. Ephesians 6:4)." He continues, "Hate in this context is a Semitic way of expressing preference. To hate one's family is to prefer God over them by disregarding what they desire if that conflicts with what God requires; it is to love God more… All other loves must be subordinate to loving God with all one's heart, soul, mind, and strength" (Luke 10:27).[81]

Practical Applications

I think it boils down to making choices based upon priorities of what people think is important. When parents choose sports, academics, employment, or lessons over God's work in and through the church, I think kids are likely to grow up with an understanding that those things may be more important than what God is doing in His church.

I grew up in a day when my parents didn't give my brothers and me a choice. We were not allowed to miss church or youth group for a part-time job, for homework, for basketball practice, or any other cultural activity. We knew that church was more important than those things, and my parents emphatically enforced that practice.

I understand that times have changed and that few parents make those kinds of choices anymore. My wife and I had to come to our own conclusions on this very issue when our children were growing up. We wanted to make intentional decisions about the choices our children made concerning sports involvement or other extra-curricular activities. Full disclosure here: we ended up not being as "legalistic" as my parents were about specific involvements in the churches we attended. But, as I mentioned in Conversation #4, we decided to make the following church "functions" as top priorities for our family and for our kids' schedules—preaching, worship, service, fellowship, evangelism, and giving.

These six priorities formed the basis for our decision making as parents. We were never the parents who acted like "whenever the church was open we had to be there." In fact, we made conscious decisions to not involve our children in some of the activities and functions in the churches we attended. But we did make the church functions that emphasized those things (preaching, worship, service, fellowship, evangelism, and giving) as very, very important for our family and for our children.

This, of course, isn't the only factor or reason that all three of our children are currently serving the Lord and have all grown up to go on for God[82] (praise the Lord!). But, I do think the choices Peggy and I made for their lives when they were children helped our kids to see that God's work—the church—is critically important and it's worth our effort to be involved in what God is doing. In fact, it is amazing to us that all of those six things are still very important in their lives. Of course, we continually praise Him for His work in and through their lives individually.

Some Practical Suggestions for Christian Parents

So, let's make this as useful and helpful as we can. Here are some simple yet practical ideas, based upon key Biblical principles, that Christian parents can insert into the life of their families:

1. Begin your parenting process by making a commitment to be involved in God's work. (See Hebrews 10:25: *"Not forsaking the assembling of ourselves together..."*) Parenting is one of the hardest and yet most rewarding tasks a person could ever have. This is especially true for Christian parents who want to raise their kids to love and serve the Lord, which is of course a Biblical mandate.[83] That's why I encourage all prospective parents, parents of young children, and parents of teenagers alike to make a personal pledge or commitment to raise their children in church. Please believe me, parents must be committed to this or it won't happen. The demands and schedules of everyday contemporary life have a way of crowding out the things that are really important. This begins with a spiritual and intellectual acknowledgement that the church is God's work and is God's plan for this age. The church is what God is doing in the world today. Even with all of the human imperfections and sinful hypocrisies that people bring to the church, it is still worth it for parents to make this a commitment for their children. Parents, if this hasn't been your practice—I urge you, begin now.

2. Make a list of the priorities you want to build into the lives of your family and your children and then be dedicated in the development of those habits in your family's schedule. (See 1 Timothy 4:7: *"...exercise yourself toward godliness."*) Even though I am a big fan of the church, I'll admit that I have seen church programming and scheduling that is excessive and maybe even quite unnecessary. As I mentioned elsewhere, my generation came of age in an over-programmed, busy-is-best

mentality in the church. For instance, when I was a youth pastor early in my ministry, our church had an event or program scheduled literally every night of the week.

Many churches recently have adopted a newer model of church programming philosophy as presented in the book *Simple Church: Returning to God's Process for Making Disciples* by Thom Rainer and Eric Geiger,[84] which I think is a balanced and appropriate approach. It's not that church is ever "simple" or easy. Quite the opposite. These authors promote the idea that the process should be simple—in other words that each local church should present clear and thorough reasons for having specific programs, events, ministries, or services.

That's exactly the approach I am advocating for parents. Christian parents should take the time to do what we did with our family. Sit down together and identify a set of Biblical priorities that they believe should be lasting, Godly habits in the lives of their individual family members.

Once that list was identified, we then made sure that the church programs our family participated in were areas where those priorities were emphasized. As I mentioned, the Sunday morning services were always a priority because we wanted Biblical, expository preaching and Christ-honoring worship to be emphasized. We also looked for ways our family members could serve the Lord together, and we definitely wanted each of our family members to develop meaningful fellowship with other Christians who were growing in Christ themselves. Providing our family with specific opportunities for outreach and evangelism, plus tithing and giving to church also became important habits for our family.

3. <u>Be consistent about implementing the same priorities in your own life</u>. (See 2 Timothy 1:5: *"When I call to remembrance the genuine faith that is in you, which dwelt first in your grandmother Lois and your mother Eunice, and I am persuaded is in you also."*) Believing parents must understand that it's not enough to make a list of priorities for our children that we are not willing to implement in our own lives. The Apostle Paul put it this way to his student Timothy, in 2 Timothy 3:14, *"You must continue in the things which you have learned and been assured of, knowing from whom you have learned them."* If we want our children to grow up with Godly habits, we must demonstrate them faithfully in our lives as well. Parents can never expect our children to grow up with practices that were never modeled for them. We've all heard the old cliché—*much more is caught than taught*. If we want these things to be priorities in the lives of our kids, the same things need to be important in our lives and schedules first.

4. <u>Make sure that your family is deliberate about the process of framing your calendar and schedule</u>. (Ephesians 5:16: *"...redeeming the time, because the days are evil."*) I want to review this suggested process for parents so far—make a commitment to be involved in church, establish a list of specific Biblical priorities you want to build into the individual lives of your family members, and be sure that those same priorities are consistently practiced in your lives as parents. This last step then is also very, very important. This plan will never work unless we are willing to manage our own family schedules as well. We all know how it goes. It's the old problem of the "tyranny of the urgent"[85]—when we allow "urgent" things to come into our lives, they crowd out the important things. We must control our calendars, which definitely includes the scheduling of cultural activities like we talked about above, as well as church events and programs. In other words, parents must learn

to be very intentional about what we schedule and plan for our children—and for our own lives as well. Life will quickly become very scattered, hectic, and frenzied unless we slow down and only allow what we have clearly identified as "important" and even essential into our schedules. This should include, of course, areas of personal disciplines, like daily time with God, Scripture memory, prayer, outreach, etc., as well as church involvement and some select and specific educational or community areas of participation that we view as strategic for our family members.

Some Practical Suggestions for Church Leaders

In the same vein as the action steps I listed above for parents, here are some practical and real-life thoughts for church leaders. I want to reemphasize something that I stated earlier: I am not trying to pass myself off as an expert on church programming or structure. I've had the opportunity to witness church trends because I have visited a wide variety of churches, and am someone who is very concerned about encouraging the next generation to grow up and go on for God.

1. Develop and publicize a clear Biblical philosophy of church functions and programming. It is absolutely essential for each church, no matter the size, to establish a specific Biblical and practical philosophy that provides a foundational reason for everything the church does. I define *philosophy* as a "set of reasons." It is why we do what we do.

   This step is imperative. People in today's busy culture with its hyperactive scheduling will find it more and more difficult to attend or participate in something that does not have a clear-cut and vital purpose for its existence. The days of people attending church because of duty or responsibility, or even because of guilt, are long gone. People in today's culture just don't attend church because they are supposed to go. In fact, one report recently revealed that 80% of all Americans do not attend church on any given weekend.[86]

Pastors, elders, and other church leaders may have their own understanding of why people should attend a certain meeting or function. They may even have a specific Biblical conviction in their own minds about why people should participate in church. But unless that reason is clearly and effectively communicated within the church itself and then to the watching community, people will not think that particular program or meeting is worth their while to attend. Maybe that's one reason for culture's lack of commitment to church attendance in today's society. People may just not fully grasp why it is so important for them to attend church functions each week.

Let me provide a personal illustration from my own ministry, which is candidly all too common in so many churches today. I was scheduled to preach in a church one Sunday, and the pastor asked me (somewhat at the last minute) if I would also be willing to speak to the teenagers in their Sunday School class that met before the church's morning service. I agreed and was told that the class began at 10:00 a.m. I arrived during a heavy rain storm about 9:45 a.m., figuring that was enough time for me to find the teen classroom, meet the teacher, and make final preparations for the meeting. I ran through the rain to the church's main door only to find it locked with no one inside to let me in. I then ran back to my car and waited a few moments for someone to show up and unlock the door. That person finally arrived and let me into an empty church building. They told me the teenagers meet for Sunday School in the church basement, and then left me on my own to find my way down a dark staircase and even darker basement hallway. The youth worker and a few young people arrived about 10:15 a.m. and the class got started a few minutes after that.

Readers, let me ask you a question. Would you want to make a commitment to that church for your family if that was how the church's leadership acted? Probably not. From all appearances, they didn't even believe that Sunday School program was important. So, why should people in that community feel any differently?

I know what many of you are thinking: That is not the picture of your church or youth ministry—and you work very hard to make it a polished, upbeat, friendly, and welcoming environment. You would have a very valid argument there, and I absolutely applaud youth workers who put a great deal of effort and planning into their programs, meetings, and activities. In fact, I would unequivocally state that most of the youth pastors and youth workers I know work very hard on their programming efforts. But please hear me out. Is your philosophy and purpose effectively communicated to your attendees and potential participants?

Church leaders must make sure that the specific reason for having a meeting or function (for example: Sunday School, small group meetings, youth group, even morning services, etc.) is clearly communicated and promoted to the community, to church attendees, to members—to everyone and in every way possible. That will help parents understand how important the functions you hold are for their children.

(I have included an interesting article on this topic in Appendix 3 from my friend and colleague with Vision For Youth, Tim Ahlgrim entitled, *I Want Busy Kids in Our Student Ministry*.)

2. <u>Remember that your main objective is to reach, teach, and disciple young people—not build attendance at a meeting</u>. I'll discuss this point in some greater detail in Conversation #9, but I want to remind church leaders that our purpose is to develop fully devoted followers of Christ, not to make sure that meetings are well attended. Contrary to how some of this book might sound, I am convinced that youth workers have endured a "bad rap" about this. But perhaps there is some truth here that would require an honest look in the mirror of self-evaluation. Historically, many, especially outsiders, have accused youth workers of being entertainment-driven or motivated by attracting crowds of teenagers to our events. However, I am not one to judge motives. For instance, I know scores of youth workers who work hard to attract teenagers to their events, not for the sake of having a large attendance, but for the honest purpose of sharing the Gospel. So if this is the driving force—to that, I shout, "Amen!" However, here is the rub in my mind that may limit our ministry's effectiveness in today's culture: Do we act like real ministry can only occur at our events or meetings? Perhaps this is why, maybe unwittingly, so many youth workers blame and criticize parents of teenagers for not supporting our programs. Possibly it's time to stop evaluating "success" in youth ministry by how many kids attend our functions, but by how effective we are at actually reaching young people for Christ and then discipling them to walk with Him over the long haul. That seems like the real mission of the church to me! I really like how author Carey Nieuwhof puts it, "More and more as a leader, I value *engagement* over attendance."[87]

I've heard many youth workers blame parents and teenagers today for being too busy, but perhaps that's our problem, too. Maybe our own schedules are too full with meetings and events that we don't really have the time for early-morning prayer times with high school athletes, to attend concerts or plays at the local high schools, or to meet individually with some of our high-achieving kids (who may not be able to attend every youth group meetings) for coffee.

We all must remember that our real objective is to reach, teach, and disciple young people. Plus, the way we connect or don't connect with parents and families will either help or greatly hinder that from happening.

3. Don't over-schedule church functions and programs. As a follow-up to the last point in this conversation, there is another important action step for church leaders that will help today's families—that is to not over-schedule activities and meetings. We must understand that our people are busy with very full calendars already. In fact, many people I've met during my travels believe they are busier than they have ever been. Church leaders must be sensitive to this phenomenon. As I mentioned earlier, it doesn't help families for churches to have a full lineup of events scheduled either all-day Sunday, most Saturdays, or virtually every evening of the week. It is my contention that many families will not respond positively to that kind of timetable. Ultimately, they're likely to drop out.

Here is a programming approach that church leaders may want to seriously consider. I have noticed a growing and helpful trend that seems to have gained traction in some churches around the country, and that is to hold key meetings or programs on a temporary or short-term basis, or that are planned in shorter durations than previous generations. In other words, many churches are using weekend retreats, or two, three, or four week series of meetings, instead of a program that is held each week all year round. For example, my wife and I have served as speakers in several weekend marriage or parenting retreats. I have also been in churches that schedule meetings on specific equipping or outreach-oriented topics on a shorter term basis like a college or university would schedule a course (e.g., a semester, a module, one-night-a-week, weekend, etc.) instead of holding Sunday School classes, for instance, every Sunday all year.

Of course, several churches have eliminated Sunday School in favor of some type of small-group ministry. The various models are many, depending upon what the church is trying to accomplish. Before I leave this topic I want to issue a loving warning to church leaders. Be careful not to trade Bible teaching programs away in favor of "fellowship" or "community." Seminary president and denominational spokesman, Dr. Albert Mohler wrote about this issue on his web site, warning that "Christians who lack Biblical knowledge are the products of churches that marginalize Biblical knowledge...The move to small group ministry has certainly increased opportunities for fellowship, but many of these groups never get beyond superficial Bible study."[88]

4. <u>Help families when scheduling church meetings and functions</u>. I also believe it is imperative in today's culture for church leaders to understand and respond creatively to the unique rhythm and calendar of the general community in which your church is located. Church leaders would do well to look into what days of the week and what time schedules would work best in their communities before launching specific programs.

For instance, when I first started as a youth pastor, we held our youth group meetings on Sunday nights. As time went on, it made sense for us to switch our youth meetings to Wednesday evenings. The church I serve in now has youth group meetings on Thursday nights.

When I served in the greater Detroit, Michigan area, we held midweek prayer meetings in the mornings because so many of our people worked the second shift in the automobile factories. When our family lived in Iowa, our church's evening services and children's programs didn't start until 7:30 p.m. so that the farmers could make use of all of the daylight out in their fields. The days of "keep people busy" church schedules are gone. The ideal time for church scheduling will vary depending upon several cultural factors that are likely to be different for each community and area.

The needs of the general area you live and serve in could dictate when specific meetings and programs are scheduled. An understanding of the rhythm of your community is imperative if your church wants to help families who may already be over-scheduled.

5. Remember, your community will have more and more people from non-traditional, weak, or dysfunctional family situations. As I have already emphasized elsewhere in this book, current sociological trends reveal a growing number of people in this culture who will represent a wide diversity of family situations. You can reread my Conversation #2 for a general listing of some current statistics facing today's church. But the point is that today's church leaders will need to face the fact that more and more people in their communities will be from non-traditional and dysfunctional family backgrounds. I believe the Bible speaks to this concern in passages like 2 Timothy 3:1-9 and Titus 2:1-10.

We'll talk more about this later, but pastors and church leaders will need to realize that this is indeed happening and should search the Scriptures and then strategize with their leadership teams for ministry and outreach ideas that will effectively reach this growing demographic cohort.[89] This fact also demonstrates the validity of an increasing lack of Biblical literacy[90] and knowledge within today's culture.

6. <u>Ask people to make personal commitments to God's mission and work</u>. Despite their busy schedules, I do believe there are parents who will make the commitment to involve their families in the church. And I believe that it's time to raise the bar of true discipleship. See passages like Luke 9:23, *"If anyone desires to come after Me, let him deny himself, and take up his cross daily, and follow Me."* And Luke 14:26, *"If anyone comes to Me and does not hate his father and mother, wife and children, brothers and sisters, yes, and his own life also, he cannot be my disciple."* Jesus definitely and emphatically taught His followers to commit!

Christianity and church life must be more than a once-a-week concert, followed by a lecture from the church stage. Today's young people, along with their families (whatever that may look like), need ministries that are committed to overcoming the matter of what youth ministry professor, Thomas Bergler calls "juvenilization"[91]—the growing crisis of spiritual immaturity that is dominating the American church. According to God's Word—both institutions (Christian parents AND the church) are responsible!

"That (the older women) admonish the young women to love their husbands, to love their children..."
Titus 2:4

Conversation #6
The "Titus 2 Principle": Why Is Mentoring So Important For the Church and For Families?

Victor Hugo, the acclaimed author of *Les Misérables,* once stated, "You can resist an invading army; but, you cannot resist an idea whose time has come."[92]

Mentoring is such an idea for the church today.

The word "mentor" supposedly originated in ancient Greek mythology. In Homer's *The Odyssey,* "Mentor" was the one entrusted with tutoring Odysseus's son and providing masculine guidance and instruction in the absence of his father who was away at war.[93] That's a fitting illustration of what true mentoring is all about.

It is my opinion that mentoring is different than discipleship. I define mentoring as caring, Godly adults taking the initiative to develop personal, growing relationships with individual younger people to encourage spiritual and personal maturity—while discipleship is an organized educational ministry that requires the discipler to teach and to do life with a specific group of followers.

The responsibility in mentoring is on the adult to show the student that he or she truly cares about them and wants to be involved tangibly in their life. The adult is the one who should most often initiate the connection because he or she sees that the student needs encouragement and guidance. Plus, it provides another level of essential inter-generational relationships in the church.

For those of us who grew up in the church, most likely our lives are lined with caring people who took the time to be personally involved with us. Do you remember the impact of loving adults in your life? They were probably people like Sunday School teachers, youth workers, or other interested adults who took the time to reach out to impressionable young people. Most often it is the little things those adults did that we remember the most.

On a personal note, my wife and I are very thankful for the caring adults in the churches we attended that took a genuine interest in the lives of our children during their years in children's ministry and in youth groups. Our children's lives are fuller because of the influence of Godly adults who cared enough to share their lives with them. We greatly appreciate the long line of other adults who cared about them individually and who steered them toward following God's leading in their lives.

I often tell people that mentoring is not necessarily a commitment of a huge amount of extra time on the part of the adult. Quite the contrary; real mentoring often involves little things like taking the time in the church foyer to meet younger people, engaging them in meaningful conversations, and then building growing relationships with them encouraging them in their own walk with the Lord.

Mentoring is simply doing what you do, just doing it with someone younger. If you serve in the church, why not recruit and train someone younger to serve alongside you? If you participate in a hobby or another area of personal interest (like golfing, hunting, working on cars, doing a craft, or going to concerts together), why not take someone younger along with you? Almost any activity can foster a mentoring relationship if it gives the older adult the opportunity to encourage younger people personally and spiritually. (For a list of additional mentoring ideas, see Appendix 2 of this book.)

Biblical Basis

One example of a clear Biblical passage that aptly describes the concept of mentoring is found in 1 Thessalonians 2:8: *"So, affectionately longing for you, we were well pleased to impart to you not only the gospel of God, but also our own lives, because you had become dear to us."* It must be noted that there are two basic priorities here of a healthy and growing mentoring relationship.

First of all, it is very important to remember that any true spiritual relationship begins with a commitment to faithfully communicate the truth of God's Word. Notice the emphasis the Apostle Paul puts in this chapter upon "the Gospel" (see 1 Thessalonians 2, verse 2, 4, 8, and 9.) Spiritual mentoring is not just developing a personal relationship between a caring adult and a maturing protégé. It is the also the obligation of the mentor to base that relationship upon the principles and precepts of God's Word. Paul himself did that during his ministry with the Thessalonian people. This point is made very clear in the account of his time in Thessalonica as recorded in Acts 17:1 – 15.

The other basic priority here is the desire on the part of the mentor to share his or her life with the student. The Apostle Paul was extremely concerned about sharing the Gospel, but he was also motivated to share his life with the Thessalonian believers as well. These two priorities form the very foundation of a God-honoring mentoring relationship. We must encourage adults to take the time to share God's Word with students, but it must be in an environment where the mentor shares his or her life as well.

Effective spiritual mentors must make a commitment to share the Word of God **and** their own lives with students. This will take some effort and energy. Paul was deeply concerned about the Thessalonian people. Notice the phrase *"we were well pleased."* It could also be translated that they were delighted or thrilled to have shared life with the Thessalonians.[94] The wording here demonstrates a constant yearning for a close, personal relationship.

Paul further illustrates what that close, personal relationship in mentoring looks like in 1 Thessalonians 2:7-12.

Paul uses two very familiar examples to help readers understand how this works: (1) <u>a loving mother</u>, verse 7; and (2) <u>a hard-working father</u>, verse 11.

It is interesting to note that Paul uses family metaphors to emphasize his love and care for the Thessalonian people. As mothers are absolutely indispensable to the growth and development of children, so can spiritual mentors be essential for the spiritual maturity of students. The Biblical language here illustrates the gentle love of a nursing mother. There is perhaps nothing as special as that kind of human relationship between a mother and infant. There is something very warm and tender about a mother's love for her children.

Paul's second illustration in this text is that of a hard-working father. Make no mistake—mentoring will require hard work, and it certainly takes adults who love students. My most vivid memory of growing up with my dad was the fact that he was a hard worker. He was not the kind of guy to sit around with nothing to do. He worked hard. His dad, my grandfather, was just like that too. What I remember most about him was his strong work ethic. Grandpa Walker faced a mandatory retirement from his work at age 65 and then got another full-time job that he held for over 20 more years until he died in his late 80s. By using the analogy of a hard-working father, Paul is making it very clear that ministering to people this way is indeed difficult. It's an illustration we can certainly understand.

The wording here also stresses that a father's role includes modeling and motivating. Notice the text in verse 11, "*...exhorted, and comforted, and charged every one of you, as a father does his own children.*" Effective mentors have this kind of ministry with young people. Notice the next verse for the purpose behind this extreme effort. Paul's goal for the Thessalonian believers must be our goal for our protégés as well. Obviously, we want them to grow up to "*walk worthy of God, who calls you*" (v. 12). Mentoring requires gentle love and hard work, but isn't this end result exactly what we want for our students as well? Mentoring can help that happen by providing the next generation in our churches with growing personal relationships with a group of Godly and caring adults.[95]

Readers will remember the important statistic I mentioned from youth ministry specialist, Dr. Chap Clark in Conversation #5, that today's teenagers need strong personal relationships with five significant adults (other than their parents) if they are going to continue involvement in church after high school graduation.[96] I really believe that an intentional, somewhat prearranged mentoring ministry can and will provide another layer of adult-to-student connections in your church. My opinion is that these Godly and caring adult mentors should be adults outside the team of specific youth workers who are already in place in your church. These are adults who are specifically praying for young people and who are taking the initiative to develop growing personal relationships with individual young people, especially those with family concerns or personal needs.

Developing a "Titus 2 Church"

Probably the most familiar passage in Scripture that clearly outlines the significance of church-based mentoring is found in Titus 2:1-8. That text encourages older people to have a positive and growing mentoring relationship with younger people in the following broad general categories: teaching of Biblical truth, the development of character qualities, people skills, family and marriage relationships, and outreach. These are the very things older people can and should teach to younger people in the church.

A "Titus 2 ministry" can certainly happen with high school students, or emerging young adults, as older, Godly people work to develop growing relationships with them. But it can also occur with older married couples reaching out to younger couples, and older parents, perhaps those whose children are beyond their teenage years, mentoring parents with young children.

Notice how this chapter begins, *"But as for you, speak the things which are proper for sound doctrine"* (v. 1). In other words, the Apostle Paul is instructing Titus to make these inter-generational connections a priority in the church. Pastors, youth pastors, and other church leaders should intentionally identify Godly adult mentors who have the ability to fulfill these instructional responsibilities in the lives of upcoming generations and do everything they can to build mentoring connections within the fabric of their church ministries.

It is a natural thing for older people to have a teaching and training ministry in the lives of younger people. The Scriptures contain multiple illustrations of specific inter-generational connections. (See the Biblical accounts of Moses with Joshua, Elijah with Elisha, and Paul with Timothy, John Mark and others.) Yet, even a quick look at history shows us that our culture has done more to separate the various age groups than at any other time.[97] Since the cultural advent of adolescence and a youth culture, we have been prone to segregate and disconnect the generations in our schools, businesses, churches, and other social institutions. Our culture divides children, youth, and adults into separate age groups that have very few connections with the other age groups.

The "Titus 2 Imperative" provides Biblical instruction that confirms this age group division was not to be the case in the church. In fact, I believe that many older people will want to have mentoring relationships with younger people—and younger people, especially today's Millennials[98] and Gen-Z'ers[99] will want to be actively mentored[100] by significant, Godly older adults. It's just that we've all grown up in a culture that tends to isolate the generations. Inter-generational mentoring will work if we give it a chance.

Paul makes it very clear here that older men and older women are to teach and model godliness in order to encourage the younger men and women in some specific areas that are mentioned in this passage. In fact, the word *"admonish"* in verse 4 could be translated "to train" or even "to encourage." Greek scholar, Kenneth S. Wuest translates it this way, "to make sane or sober-minded, to recall a person to his senses."[101]

There is something very special about inter-generational mentoring relationships. Older women can and should train and encourage younger women; likewise, older men can train and encourage younger men. This is how the church is supposed to work.

How to Develop Mentoring Connections in Your Church

So, let's make this as practical as we can. Here are some basic principles to consider as you encourage the Godly, older adults in your church to develop healthy and growing mentoring relationships with younger people.

1. <u>Pray that the Lord would give significant, older adults a burden for specific younger people</u>. The entire mentoring process must be bathed in prayer. Please do not ignore this important first step. I honestly believe that a great deal of the tension and arguments in churches over external matters, such as tastes in fashion or music styles, would be obliterated if the older, mature, Godly believers were praying intentionally, fervently, and individually for the younger, emerging generations in the church. Plus, I think the young adults are more likely to stay in a church rather than walk away if they know that the older generations are praying specifically for them **by name**!

   Let me summarize this very practical advice here to all church leaders and Christian parents alike: get older, Godly people praying specifically, by name, for your kids!

2. <u>Prospective mentors should look for younger people with specific needs and for those who just need encouragement</u>. As Christ tarries before His return, it will be more and more imperative for His church to operate as a family. We'll talk more specifically about this in Conversation #10, but today's culture is becoming increasingly unfriendly and even hostile toward the family. Fewer people are actually getting married, more and more people are getting married later in life, the traditional definition of marriage is changing,

dysfunctional family situations are rampant, many Christian parents (even though they may have good intentions) are busier than ever before,[102] plus our Adversary, the Devil,[103] has in a sense declared war against Christian parents who are doing all they can to raise their own children to grow up and go on for God. In this culture, it will be absolutely imperative for the church to be a family—actively welcoming, teaching, admonishing, accepting, and loving more and more people from incredibly difficult home situations and encouraging them to be a part of the true fellowship that a loving and caring local church should provide.

Godly, spiritually-mature older adults who are interested in mentoring younger people must especially be on the lookout for those from needy family backgrounds. Plus, we cannot assume that young people from theoretically "good, Christian families" do not need mentors. I believe that all Christian young people need the Godly influence of several adults in the church who are lovingly and totally committed to encouraging them toward spiritual maturity. The Biblical pattern is for the larger body of Christ to provide older, mature examples of what it means to follow Christ faithfully over time. (See Barnabas with Saul and then John Mark, Paul with Silas, Timothy, Luke, and many others—and even Christ with His disciples.)

3. <u>Effective mentors often have much in common with specific younger people</u>. Usually the best mentors are people with something in common with those they are mentoring. Wise church leaders will work within their congregations to find potential older mentors who can identify the things they have in common with specific younger people in need. This might simply mean they already know them somehow. It might be that they live geographically near them, or have vocational interests alike. Maybe there are hobbies, crafts, or activities they

have in common; or perhaps they may have similar personal life experiences.

Later on in this chapter we'll talk about Barnabas and his mentoring role in the early church seen in Acts 11:19-26. One of the reasons he was so effective there in Antioch was that he had so much in common with the people. Having some areas of commonality with specific younger people can be a huge advantage in a mentoring relationship.

4. <u>The best mentoring often takes place within the existing church structure</u>. If you take the time to Google the word "mentoring," you will find millions of sites that feature this concept in educational settings and millions more sites touting this idea in the business world. However, I believe that the very best mentoring takes place in the local church. In fact, mentoring actually begins in the church foyer where Godly, older adults take the initiative to launch positive and non-threatening conversations with younger people and then slowly turn those opening conversations into growing, healthy relationships.

    Plus if I had my way, or if I had the ability to make some sort of executive order on this, I would mandate or require all church ministry positions to include a mentoring piece as well. Ushers would have to mentor younger ushers, Sunday School teachers would mentor younger teachers, older deacons would mentor younger deacons, and so on. The existing structure of your local church provides an ideal launching pad for this kind of inter-generational ministry.

5. <u>Mentors should start slowly and to begin building these relationships in public, non-threatening places</u>. In today's culture, it is very, very necessary for all adults who desire to build interpersonal relationships with juveniles to obey the law as required in your particular

state. This may include doing background checks, even finger printing, and other legal clearances. Church leaders must do their homework on this issue, and parents must absolutely insist that the children's workers and youth workers in their churches go through these essential background checks. The personal and spiritual safety of the next generation is vitally important.

That being said, even with all of this accomplished, adult mentors should always, always meet with the people they are mentoring in public, non-threatening locations. This important policy is another way the church provides an accountability of protection for mentors and their protégés.

There's another issue involved here that merits some consideration as we institute a mentoring ministry. We must remember when dealing with children and adolescents that they are minors—which means that they are living under the authority of parents or another guardian. Church leaders must not usurp the rights or roles of parents, but instead should work alongside parents or other people in authority for the spiritual well-being and growth of the kids. The same basic rule-of-thumb applies in other mentoring situations as well. Mentors should always remember that their connections with others should never get in the way of other important relationships. For instance, it's a good thing for older women to mentor younger women, but never at the expense of their own husband or children.

6. Once the relationship is established, then they can work out the details of when to get together. The process of building mentoring relationships is relatively simple. It only makes sense for the potential adult mentor to initiate the connection in the foyer, and then as the relationship grows, other meeting times and places can be arranged and the details worked out. A level of

familiarity and trust needs to be established first. Once that happens, then other times to get together can be set. For example, a time for a round of golf, eating at the student's favorite restaurant, etc. (For more examples of how mentoring connections could work, see the "Mentoring Ideas Chart" in Appendix 2 of this book.)

7. <u>The mentors should always looks for opportunities to guide the conversations toward spiritual matters</u>. It's important to reemphasize here that mentoring is not just adults hanging out with teenagers, or older people developing friendships with younger people. This is ministry—it is a spiritual commitment with the purpose of helping the protégé grow toward spiritual maturity. There are other benefits to be sure, but the focus should be on spiritual growth.

Some Cautions

In addition to the simple principles I presented above, it is also important to realize there are some cautions or restraints that should be built into a mentoring ministry. I will list the ones that I've already mentioned and then share a few others.

1. The local church provides a level of accountability that is so important in today's sinful society. Church-based mentoring can be very effective, and these relationships can grow into very significant and life-changing ministries. But wise mentors will build these inter-generational relationship with the knowledge and involvement of the leaders of the church and/or youth ministry. Simply put, please let someone in leadership in the church know what you are doing.

2. Older adult mentors should remember to work within the God-given authority structure that is already in place. This includes parents or guardians of minors (even those from poor, weak, or highly dysfunctional family

situations), and could include the spouse of a younger married person.

3. Another caution to remember is the matter of time. It is very easy for loving, caring people to spend too much time with the people they are mentoring and in the process hurt or damage their own spouse or children. This is exactly why I believe a successful mentoring relationship is not necessarily a commitment of **extra** time. Again, the genius of mentoring is that growing relationships can be developed through daily life experiences. Again, it is indeed doing what you do, just doing that with someone younger.

4. This last caution may be the most important: mentors must remember to focus, first and foremost, on their own walk with God. The entire process of mentoring in a local church setting must be a spiritual exercise. The only way an older adult can truly be effective as a mentor is if the relationship is pointed directly at Jesus Christ. You'll note this fact specifically in the Biblical illustration of Barnabas and Saul below. They did not reproduce their own lives or personalities in the people they mentored. The point of their inter-generational relationships was to display or demonstrate Christ to the people they were mentoring. We must do the same!

Barnabas and the Biblical Characteristics of Effective Mentors

Take a few minutes right now to read Acts 11:19-26. It is the Scriptural account of the amazing growth of the church at Antioch that happened when the new believers scattered there following the martyrdom of Stephen (see Acts 7:54-60). By the time we get to this text in Acts 11, Saul, a former leader of the persecution of Christ followers (see Acts 8:1), had come to Christ on the Damascus Road (see Acts 9:1-30), had been briefly mentored by the church leaders in Jerusalem, such as Ananias and Barnabas (see Acts 9:10-30), and had returned to his home town of Tarsus (see Acts 9:30 and Acts 11:25), undoubtedly awaiting a new ministry assignment from God.

During that time, Barnabas was unquestionably one of the key figures in the early church (see Acts 4:36-37 and Acts 9:27). The designation "Barnabas" was actually a nickname of sorts. His given name was Joseph (see Acts 4:36). The moniker Barnabas was bestowed on him by other church leaders because of his natural propensity to be an encouragement to everyone around him. He is originally introduced to us in Acts 4:36-37 as a man of genuine integrity and generosity. It makes great sense that he was the one the Jerusalem church sent on to Antioch (see Acts 11:22) to encourage and instruct the new converts who were gathering there.

This narrative (Acts 11:19-26) contains a wealth of very practical characteristics for what a church-based mentoring initiative looks like in everyday, real-world environments.

1. **Barnabas was accountable**. Notice that *"the church in Jerusalem"* (v. 22) sent Barnabas to Antioch. He was under their accountably and their authority. This was not a random act. The word *"sent"* implies purposeful activity—and ultimately he reported back to the Jerusalem church what was happening in Antioch (see Acts 11:30). This is one reason why I am such a supporter of church-based mentoring. The local church provides the structure and the community that is required of a truly effective mentoring ministry. Plus, the public aspect of the local church being involved is also important for genuine mentoring relationships to develop. I think this is the genius behind the classic church-based mentoring system that the Apostle Paul taught in Titus 2. I believe these passages indicate a structure of sorts—that inter-generational relationships should be developed, but within an intentional, church-wide format.

2. **Barnabas was a mature Christian.** By this time in the Biblical account of his life, Barnabas was already a seasoned and experienced leader in the early church.

Among other experiences, he was greatly used by God to mentor Saul (see Acts 9:27) by helping this young convert get assimilated into the church community. He was the ideal person to help these new believers in Antioch grow in Christ. This is an imperative in a truly effective mentoring relationship. Mentors must be spiritually mature and must be Godly examples to the younger, less mature believers.

3. **Mentoring is about having things in common.** A little background information is in order here to fully appreciate this story. This background material may explain why it was so strategic for the Jerusalem church leaders to send Barnabas as a mentor to the people at Antioch. This passage points out that some of the new believers in the Antioch church were actually men from Cyprus (see verses 19 and 20). This is quite interesting when we realize that Barnabas too was actually from Cyprus (see Acts 4:26). Barnabas could connect with them because he certainly had things in common with them. That is a key ingredient in any mentoring relationship. Ministry is much more effective when the mentors' backgrounds are similar to the people they are mentoring.

4. **Barnabas was an encourager.** This point perhaps seems obvious in the flow of this book, but it needs to be emphasized. Barnabas *"encouraged them all"* (Acts 11:23). It's a rare quality to be able to have that kind of positive influence on everyone; but that's how God used him. And note what Barnabas did specifically—he *"encouraged them all that with purpose of heart they should go on for God."*[104] This isn't a description of a "power-of-positive-thinking," eternal optimist, or Joel Osteen/Robert Schuller type of person. Quite the contrary. This verse depicts the ministry of someone who was used of God to exhort others to go on for God. Today's young people need adults like this in their lives—older, Godly, more

mature encouragers to motivate them in their own walk with Christ.

I want to make a sub-point here that could be filed under the "this should be obvious" category, but it needs to be emphasized from this passage and also in our churches. Young people and younger believers desperately need encouragers. I have noticed that there are way too may discouragers in the body of Christ today. I get it that not everyone has a "rah-rah," cheerleader-type personality, and not everyone is an extrovert. But please don't put discouragers around young people. The next generation needs more people like Barnabas—they need encouragers.

5. **Barnabas was intentional about mentoring.** The intentionality in the passage is obvious, and should be motivating as well. The Jerusalem church sent Barnabas to Antioch, and he had an incredible ministry there (see v. 24) so that *"a great many people were added to the Lord."* But then, right in the middle of all the great things God was doing there, the text tells us that Barnabas *"departed for Tarsus to seek for Saul"* (v. 25). Barnabas was wise enough, mature enough, and serious enough about these new converts in Antioch that he knew they needed someone else with a different set of gifts and abilities in their lives. Barnabas immediately thought of Saul—the new convert he had personally mentored earlier. So Barnabas left the activity there in Antioch to make this trip back to Saul's hometown to recruit him to join the team in the work at Antioch. That is exactly what good mentors do—they get other people involved in the process. Effective mentoring relationships are often somewhat fluid as different people within the body of Christ perform a variety of ministries with a variety of different people. (By the way, this is a good picture of the church utilizing people with various spiritual gifts as described in 1 Corinthians 12.)

6. **The ministry was Bible-centered**. There was a certain focus to the ministry of Barnabas and Saul, whom he had strategically partnered with in this mentoring ministry in Antioch, and that was their emphasis upon teaching the Scriptures. Verse 26 puts it this way, *"They assembled with the church and taught a great many people."* This phrase also implies a purposefulness to their ministry. It wasn't a hap-hazard, informal relationship. These young converts needed to be grounded in the Scriptures, and the Lord gave Barnabas and Saul the opportunity to do just that. Building growing personal, inter-generational relationships is imperative in any mentoring connection, but this process must be much more than just hanging out together. We must not forget that the goal here was spiritual maturity, and that hasn't changed over the centuries. God's Word makes that obvious in passages like 2 Timothy 3:16-17, Ephesians 4:11-16, and Colossians 2:6-8. The clear, complete teaching of the Scriptures is essential for spiritual growth.

I love the passage in Luke 24:13-35. Christ, in one of His post-resurrection appearances to His disciples, walked with them on their journey to Emmaus. Verse 32 says, *"Did not our heart burn within us while He talked with us on the road, and while He opened the Scriptures to us?"* This is an apt illustration of ministry—He walked with them and opened the Scriptures. We should look for every opportunity to do the same thing.

7. **Mentoring takes some time.** Spending time together is another practical aspect of any mentoring relationship. Notice this phrase in verse 26, *"for a whole year they assembled with the church..."* Obviously, this is also very important. Real ministry cannot happen without spending some time together—and this will probably be a huge issue in today's culture. I have talked about this elsewhere in this book. People are so busy. That's why I often remind people that true mentoring is not

necessarily a commitment of *extra* time. Instead, like I mentioned, *it is doing what you do, just doing it with someone younger*. An effective mentoring ministry must flow out of a genuine lifestyle of living consistently for Him.

The story of Barnabas and Saul's ministry in Antioch continues in verse 30 of Acts 11 with the notation that the church in Antioch sent a relief offering to the believers living through a serious famine in the land of Judea. Notice that they *"sent it to the elders by the hands of Barnabas and Saul."* This, too, is an important aspect of church-based mentoring. These two men were involved in a ministry project together. They didn't just hang out together. They kept busy meeting with the church people, teaching them the Scriptures, and then delivering this relief offering (see verse 26 and 30).

8. **Their ministry was Christ-focused.** The final principle I want readers to notice here is this: Real ministry is not self-focused (either on the mentor or on the person being mentored). It is significant to note that Barnabas and Saul did not make their work in Antioch about themselves as individuals. Notice this key phrase in verse 26, *"And the disciples were first called Christians in Antioch."* Their ministry there was so Christ-focused that they produced *disciples* (followers of Christ) who were so Christ-like that they were actually called "little Christs" (or *Christians)* by the unsaved people there in Antioch. This is amazing to me. The converts didn't become like Barnabas or like Saul necessarily—they became like Christ. I think this is the same idea in 1 Corinthians 11:1 when Paul told his readers, *"Imitate me, just as I also imitate Christ."*

Encouraging young people to become mature followers of Christ is what true mentoring is all about!

"And Jesus increased in wisdom and stature, and in favor with God and men." Luke 2:52

Conversation #7
Collaboration: How Can the Church and Home Work Together For the Same Purpose?

The basic premise of this book is simple: Christian parents are responsible to raise their children to spiritual maturity (see Ephesians 6:1-4) and the church exists to reach people for Christ and to disciple them to become "fully devoted followers of Christ"[105] (see Ephesians 4:11-16). Both of these God-given institutions have the same grand purpose—encouraging the next generation to grow up and go on for God.

It only makes sense then for the two institutions to collaborate for the long-term good of the next generation.

Over the last several years, there seems to be a resurgence of interest in the idea that churches should work *with* the family for the spiritual benefit of the kids. This is the purpose of current ministry organizations such as the *Orange/reThink* movement, established by Reggie Joiner, who was also one of the founding pastors, along with Andy Stanley, of North Point Community Church near Atlanta, Georgia. Joiner compellingly asks, "What if the church and the home combined their efforts and began to work off the same page for the sake of the children?" He goes on to say that a true merger of the church and the home would have a "potentially revolutionary effect" on the lives of children.[106]

The following outline is referred to as the "Orange Strategy"—which correctly explains and identifies the logical progression in the following statements: (1) Nothing is more important than someone's relationship with God; (2) No one has more potential influence in a child's relationship with God than a parent; (3) No one has more potential to influence the parent than the church; (4) The church's potential to influence a child dramatically increases when it partners with a parent; and (5) The parent's potential to influence a child dramatically increases when that parent partners with the church.[107]

This philosophic trend has spawned other ministry leaders and organizations with a similar focus, such as *D6* (based on the principles found in Deuteronomy 6:1-9) organized by Ron Hunter, Jr.,[108] *YouthBuilders* directed by Dr. Jim Burns,[109] the *Center for Parent Youth Understanding* led by Dr. Walt Mueller, and *Legacy Milestones* with Brian Haynes.[110] But perhaps the person most credited with the resurgence of the philosophy that church leaders should work *with* Christian parents and families has been Mark DeVries from his book *Family-Based Youth Ministry: Reaching the Been-There, Done-That Generation*, which was originally published in 1994.

Before that time, the basic tendency in most youth ministries was to feature programs and events that attracted teenagers themselves, almost as "free agents." That approach was generated out of an ever-expanding youth culture that had permeated American thought since the mid-1940s.[111]

The new trend to see teenagers, not as independent beings, but as living under the authority and responsibility of their parents has definitely made a revival in today's local church youth ministry. In other words, many churches now look at youth ministry as part of an overall family ministry. In fact, more and more churches seem to be hiring "family pastors" in the place of youth pastors that had been the staffing priority for several prior decades.[112] (However, even though it is a growing trend for churches to call the role a "family pastor," I am not convinced that the majority do so with a full Biblical and philosophical understanding of that position's role and responsibility within the local church community. We'll discuss more about family ministry later on in this chapter.)

My travels have led me to a greater appreciation for local churches. However, it has been my experience that "family ministry" has now become a fashionable trend in today's church. The predisposition to reach out to teenagers as a separate demographic seems to be changing in the American church. It perhaps has been replaced by a desire to minister to the entire family unit—working with and through parents to foster greater access and effectiveness in the homes of church people. Programming for evangelism has been exchanged for ministering to people who are already a part of the church.

I definitely applaud this trend toward a holistic approach to reaching and discipling teenagers. We all must understand and appreciate the fact that teens are indeed *minors*, living under the authority of their parents or legal guardians. Which means that truly effective youth ministry must include a strategic approach that identifies parents as the ones *primarily* responsible for the maturation process of their children through adolescence into adulthood. It has been my observation that many church leaders are now recognizing the overall responsibility parents have for their children.

This important fact, however, must not discount three other significant realities: (1) the local church also has a Biblical responsibility for the spiritual maturation of its people;[113] (2) more and more people today will be from dysfunctional, non-traditional, non-Christian, or weak home environments;[114] and (3) as churches reach out to their communities,[115] it is still true that children and young people will come to Christ by the grace of God, with or without their parents' involvement. In other words, youth evangelism still works.

The historical fact that the discipline of youth ministry was birthed out of a compelling desire to reach teenagers for Christ[116] gives credence to the lasting value of outreach to teenagers as a top priority. According to the Barna Group, "nearly half of all Americans who accept Jesus Christ as their Savior do so before reaching the age of 13 (43%), and that two out of three born again Christians (64%) made that commitment to Christ before their 18th birthday."[117]

The research has been done. As one author wrote, "There is a much greater chance kids will stay connected to God as faith is modeled and talked about at home."[118] And another stated, "The most important social influence in shaping young people's religious lives is the religious life modeled and taught to them by their parents."[119] Obviously, parents living a consistent Christian life at home is definitely a catalyst for long-term spiritual maturity. However, we must not forget that God's *amazing grace* is what compels people to Christ.[120] In other words, in spite of any pattern of human sin, parental dysfunction, or changing cultural definitions in the home, God can and will obviously and absolutely use His Word and His church to help people go on for Himself.

Family Ministry in the Church Overview

The current inclination for children's ministry and youth ministry to embrace *family ministry* however has taken on several quite polarizing positions. In many cases this trend toward family ministry is a positive one for the church in that parents are being recognized as having the ultimate responsibility for their children. On the other hand, I'm not sure this trend totally takes into account the fact that the family, as a stable and spiritually-healthy institution, is actually in serious decline in this country. At the time when many churches are seeing parents as the most important influence for positive spiritual formation, the trend is actually moving in the exact opposite direction. It behooves church leaders to search the Scriptures, pray intently and specifically, study the demographics of your area, and research the various viewpoints[121] that are out there before adopting a ministry programming strategy that may be trendy, but that may not fit the needs of your church or community.

In my travels to churches, I've observed a wide range of philosophic perspectives in the family ministry continuum. At one end of the spectrum is what I call the "absentee parent" approach, which means that for whatever reason, the parents are not involved in the spiritual lives of their kids. This could mean the parents are literally, physically not present; or it could be because they are unsaved and have no interest in the spiritual development of their kids. Churches that reach out to this clientele often do so with an evangelistic approach to youth ministry that seeks to reach teenagers for Christ.

At the other end of the scale would be the "family-integrated church" movement—a philosophy that teaches that parents are totally responsible for the spiritual well-being of their kids, and that presents the idea that the church only exists to equip parents (especially fathers) to be the spiritual "heads" of their homes.[122] It is here where I would position the parents who tout the idea that they are to be the *primary disciplers* of their own kids.[123]

As I mention elsewhere in this book, I have met several Christian parents who believe they are the only ones who can and should influence their kids. My description here of this approach may be somewhat of an exaggeration, but over the last few years, I have heard multiple parents verbally defend this basic attitude toward the church youth ministry.

The following chart and commentary contain a simplistic overview of some of the various approaches toward family ministry in the church. I will definitely admit that this synopsis is a "30,000-foot look" and an over-simplified review of some of the trends I have observed in churches during my travels. This is not intended to serve as a primer to assist church leaders to embrace or launch any one particular philosophy. I will however be honest with my own assessment of each perspective.

1. <u>Parents Are Absent</u>. Some churches understand the importance of an evangelistic outreach to teenagers in their communities and work hard to have a missional emphasis through their youth ministry. This sometimes includes ways to invest in the public school system, or through programs and events that attract unsaved kids so that they hear the Gospel and come to Christ. The result is the opportunity for churches to develop a plan

to reach out to the unbelieving parents as well. In the meantime, these churches can provide caring and Godly adult mentors to help assimilate the newly saved teenagers into the local body.[124]

ROLE OF PARENTS	ROLE OF YOUTH MINISTRY	RESULT
Parents Are Absent	Share the Gospel & Provide Spiritual Mentors	Kids See the Gospel in Action from Loving Adults
Parents Are Disinterested	Significant Spiritual Influence	Kids Are Welcomed and See Church as a Family
Parents Bring Their Children	Responsibility for Spiritual Input & Social Connections	Church Leaders Teach God's Word & Reach Out to Families
Parents Who Serve	Utilize Parents to Help in Church Ministry	Kids See Parents as Willing Helpers
Parents Learn From Church Leaders	Church Leaders Hold Classes to Teach Parents	Parents Learn About Youth Culture & Some Parenting Skills
Parents Collaborate With Church Leaders	Work Alongside Parents to Encourage Toward Spiritual Maturity	Kids Grow Spiritually and Many Go On For God
Parents Mentor Other Parents	Equip Older Parents to Mentor Younger Parents	Kids Learn That Parents Need Input from Others in the Church
Parents Disciple Their Own Children	Stay Out of the Way	Kids Are Isolated From Broader Christian Community

2. <u>Parents Are Disinterested</u>. Some churches reach out to young people from families with parents who in practice seem quite disinterested in the activities of their children. These parents would be the opposite of "Helicopter Parents"[125] (those are the parents that *hover* over their kids and who are very overprotective). There are a large number of parents today who seem to be uncaring and uninvolved in the lives of their offspring. I've visited some churches that work hard to identify and recruit a number of Godly adults who would be willing to serve as almost surrogate "parents" or as potential "big brothers or big sisters" (we'll talk more about this in Conversation #9) and seek to have an influence on their lives through developing inter-generational connections.

3. <u>Parents Bring Their Children to Church Functions</u>. There are other churches that only seem to minister to the families that bring their kids to church. This is what I call the "VBS mentality"—hosting traditional children's programs during the summer for the children of church members instead of working hard to ensure that unsaved and unchurched kids attend. These churches seemingly are not really interested in outreach. They provide programming for church families only—content in this basic level of engagement with the church's youth ministry. The churches in this category also seem to do very little to equip or train parents for any other greater purpose. These parents look to the church's adult youth workers to provide social and spiritual outlets for their kids—and that is good enough for them.

4. <u>Parents Who Serve</u>. A large number of the churches I visited utilized parents of teenagers as helpers in various aspects of the youth ministry.[126] I've seen parents who were utilized, for instance, as chaperones, drivers, cooks, hosts, decorators, guest speakers, on prayer teams, as providers of resources, and as small group facilitators. This is a good place to start and gives the parents purpose and identity as they have the opportunity serve the Lord with their God-given gifts, skills, abilities, and resources. Identifying service-level duties for parents of teenagers provides them with hands-on ways to be involved without jumping through the hoops that may be required for a deeper level of engagement. For example, regular volunteer youth workers will need background checks and legal clearances for ongoing involvement in the youth ministry. However, parents who are utilized to decorate the meeting room or to cook for a youth event may not need that level of investigation.

5. <u>Parents Learn From Church Leaders</u>. Other churches see it as their responsibility to teach parents *how to parent*.

These churches offer family counseling, classes, seminars, and provide other resources to help parents in their communities. I visited one church that offered a wide range of family and parenting courses during their *Awana* children's program. Another offered a full curriculum of classes during that church's Sunday School program. The church leaders in this category seemed to look at their pastors and elders as *experts*, with the knowledge and/or experience to lead the educational or training sessions. This perspective is often true with churches that offer a substantial family counseling program. The church leaders have the training and expertise, so they are deemed to have *the* answers to share with needy and hurting families.

6. <u>Parents Collaborate With Church Leaders</u>. I've been in other churches where the youth and children's ministry workers see Christian parents as allies[127] or partners[128] with the church ministries.[129] This perspective promotes the idea that the church youth ministry should support parents in what they are doing with their children. That assistance often takes the form of communication pieces, semi-regular informational meetings, plus a few classes, workshops, or seminars. This perspective is where so many churches today are landing as they embrace the *Orange*[130] philosophy, *D6*[131] (from Deuteronomy 6), or *Legacy Milestones*.[132] There is a great deal of merit to this viewpoint in that it provides practical ways for the two institutions (the home and the church) to collaborate with each other.

7. <u>Parents Mentor Other Parents</u>. Take a moment here to review Conversation #6 in this book. I outline there the importance and the process involved of incorporating the "Titus 2 imperative" into the life of a church. I've visited churches that do this very well. They work hard to identify and equip older parents to build growing mentoring relationships with younger parents in the

church. This approach is Biblical and it makes a great deal of sense. It allows Godly parents that have already raised their own kids (with the resulting successes and failures) to build intentional connections with younger parents who desperately need to learn from their wisdom and experience. So many churches keep young couples together, parents of teenagers together, and then older couples together in their programming efforts in a one-generational approach, when the Bible clearly teaches an inter-generational perspective in Titus 2:1-10 instead.

8. <u>Parents Disciple Their Own Children</u>. On the far end of this family ministry continuum is the *family-integrated*[133] approach I referred to earlier. This position places Christian parents as the *primary disciplers* of their own children and downplays or negates the role of church youth workers. Authors such as Voddie Baucham, J. Mark Fox, and Scott Brown are some of the leading proponents of this viewpoint. They believe that all age-segregated ministries should be eliminated in favor of families meeting together; and they teach that the practice of youth ministry is sinful and is a very negative influence on the family unit.[134]

Personally, I find important strengths and human weaknesses in all eight family ministry perspectives I have listed here. I greatly appreciate churches that are working hard to share the Gospel with unsaved people in their communities, and that approach will tend to reach people for Christ from incredibly needy households. I also applaud churches that are diligent about equipping Christian parents to be spiritual leaders in their own homes. However, the Lord has put a growing burden on my heart to encourage Christian parents to *work with the church* for the long-term spiritual success of their children **AND** to challenge churches to *be a family* in God's grand mission.

A Balance is Best

The current emphasis on family ministries in the church includes a wide array of philosophies and approaches. As I described above, the extremes range from a total emphasis upon evangelism—where youth workers develop methodologies to reach out to unsaved, unchurched families to share the Gospel; to the family-integrated model, where Christian parents have total responsibility to help their children grow spiritually and where youth workers are not involved at all. In the first approach, the parents are absent and teenagers are the focus; in the latter, adult youth workers are absent and are not needed.

I contend that truly effective family ministry is probably somewhere in the middle of those two extremes. As I visited churches, I observed all of the varieties that I highlighted in the above chart and the descriptions following. Some churches emphasized outreach to teenagers to the exclusion of their parents, which I think is a philosophical and programming error. Churches at the other end of the scale choose to concentrate on strong Christian parents as the exclusive conduit to their children—which in my opinion is a cultural and logical mistake. Proverbs 11:1 is worth considering here in an attempt to find a Biblical and practical balance in this discussion of family ministry, *"A just weight is His delight."*

If we keep in mind that both Christian parents and the church exist to encourage the next generation to grow up and go on for God,[135] then I believe there are four essential quadrants in a balanced approach to local church family ministry.

1. Outreach. If one were to do a demographics study of most American communities, most likely family issues and family concerns would top the list of needs. This presents a prime opportunity for churches today to utilize their programs and facilities as an evangelistic outreach. Plus, as churches follow the Great Commission's mandate of reaching out in ever-widening cultural circles like is depicted in Acts 1:8, undoubtedly marriage and family issues will be at the forefront of successful outreach. In other

words, in Bible times, city life in Jerusalem was quite different than the practices of their cross-cultural neighbors in Samaria. Many churches today are effectively using family ministries as a way to reach out into their communities, and rightfully so. As social changes face the church in today's culture, church leaders can respond with sensitivity, love, and awareness by developing and implementing programs, functions, and events that are geared toward the real family-related trends of their communities. For instance, how many households in your community are headed by single adults? Or what is the average age of people getting married in your community? Knowing the community's demographic trends will help church leaders as they develop new outreach initiatives. A balanced approach to family ministry must include evangelism as a top priority.

2. <u>Collaboration</u>. The purpose of this particular chapter is to motivate church leaders and Christian parents to work together for the eternal benefit of the next generation. Again, it is essential to keep God's objective in mind—we want our kids to become fully-devoted followers of Christ. And since both God-ordained institutions (the church and the home) have matching purposes, why not work together? Christian parents must be supportive of the church, and church leaders must be sensitive and proactive in their programming efforts toward the family. As I indicated earlier, this approach (church leaders working **with** Christian parents) is not necessarily in conflict with the fact that more and more households today will be inhabited by people in non-traditional roles. As Christian parents see the importance of the church and church functions, and as church leaders see the importance of reaching out and ministering to people in very real cultural settings, there is a greater

likelihood that people will grow in Christ and be equipped to effectively serve Him.

3. Equipping. The emphasis in the Ephesians 4:11-16 passage I refer to so often in this book is that the church exists to *equip* God's people for "the work of ministry,"[136] which in turn builds up the body of Christ. God uses "pastor-teachers"[137] to perfect,[138] or to train or prepare God's people to serve Him, which means to use their gifts, talents, and abilities, with the attitude[139] that they'd be willing to do anything they can to serve Him. I have often wondered why *equipping* ministries are such a weak area within local church programming since the Bible clearly lists that as a key priority for pastors in Ephesians 4. It has been my observation that many churches today gather God's people for worship, teaching/preaching, giving, and fellowship, and that today's church is fairly strong in service and perhaps, evangelism. But personally, I have not witnessed *equipping for works of ministry* as a top scheduling priority. Maybe that is because we're not sure of what an equipping ministry would look like. However, it makes practical sense for churches to look at an equipping ministry for parents as something that is very necessary. More churches would do well to plan out a training curriculum of sorts that would help parents be stronger, Godly parents. Parenting is too important to be treated so haphazardly by the church.

4. Mentoring. A fourth area of emphasis in a balanced approach to family ministry is to develop and implement an intentional mentoring ministry. Older people should be motivated to take the initiative to build growing relationships with younger people, as God's people are instructed to do in Titus 2. (I have included much more information and several

practical suggestions about church-based mentoring in Conversation #6 in this book.)

BALANCED FAMILY MINISTRY

OUTREACH	**EQUIPPING**
COLLABORATION	**MENTORING**

What Parents Want From the Church

There is one final area of this discussion I want to address before we move off of the topic of family ministry in the church. The Lord has given my wife and me the opportunity to lead a number of seminars and workshops over the past several years for parents of teenagers and preteens. We surveyed hundreds of these parents in churches of various sizes all across the country and asked them what they wanted from their local church. This information convinced us that many parents are looking for the following four things from the church:

Communication

Parents of teenagers want to know what's going on in the youth ministry. Make sure to communicate well and in every way possible—that will give them the confidence they need in you and your ministry. Don't assume teens will get the information to their parents. This is your responsibility. Utilize your church or youth group website, e-mail, mass texting, newsletters, the church bulletin, announcements, phone calls, posters, printed flyers or postcards and all other means of communication at your disposal to get the necessary information to parents. I know several youth workers who schedule regular informational meetings with parents so they do not have an excuse for not knowing what the youth ministry is doing.

Here are some things parents are likely to want to know:

- **WHY?** Begin the communication process by making sure everyone connected with your church hears your philosophy of ministry, over and over again. I define *philosophy* as a statement describing what you are trying to do and how you are proposing to do it. It should be based upon specific Biblical principles and should be very practical in nature. This is your declaration of *reasons* — again, it is WHY you do what you do. I am also a strong advocate that the basic philosophy of the children's ministry and youth ministry should be a duplicate of your entire church's philosophy of ministry, but perhaps with language somewhat different to be applicable to the various age groups.

- **WHO?** Give them basic, personal information about you and your staff, including how they can communicate with the church leadership and ministry staff members. (It will also be important for them to know your church's child protection policies and that all adult youth workers have their legal clearances.) Parents will want to know who is working with their kids.

- **WHAT?** I advise youth workers to let parents know what you are teaching their kids, and what you are doing with their kids. They'll want to know a general overview of your teaching curriculum and your program.

- **WHEN?** It's also important for church leaders to publicize their ministry calendars. Parents will want to know what time events begin and conclude, and at what time their children will be returning to the church or home after activities.

Training

Parenting is a difficult task even for the best of parents. It seems ridiculous to me that churches don't make training for parents more of a priority. This responsibility is one of the most important tasks we face, and yet we often go into parenting so unprepared. It has also been reported that church growth guru George Barna once stated that parenting classes might be the most effective means of community outreach in contemporary culture. It is no wonder, then, that so many parents of teenagers have told us that they wish their churches would provide specific means of training.

There is a very real tension here, though, because many church youth workers are younger than the parents of teenagers. I personally faced this apprehension as a young youth pastor, right out of college and trying to relate to the parent of teens and preteens in my church. I discovered that I could talk to them about the big picture of youth ministry without trying to state that I was some kind of expert on being a parent of teenagers. Frankly, I didn't have a clue how to be a parent then, but I did come in contact with several teenagers in church each week, and I also made weekly visits to multiple high schools in our area. I couldn't tell them about how to raise their own kids, but I could share my own observations and conclusions about teenagers in general and the overall picture of youth culture.

I came to the conclusion that I couldn't provide specific training on how to be a parent of teenagers, but I could make other "experts" available to them. So, I utilized our lead pastor (he and his wife had grown kids) and other adults with parenting credibility in our church and asked them to lead parenting classes and workshops for younger parents. We also brought in outside parenting specialists for training and provided other training tools for parents to utilize on their own.

Fellowship

The third thing parents need from church is fellowship. I believe that parents of teenagers desperately need fellowship and interaction with other parents of teenagers to show them that they're not in this alone. They also need fellowship with people from other age groups as well, especially with parents who have already raised their own children. Wise youth workers will help parents make these kinds of connections through various inter-generational church programs and ministries.

I want to share another idea with you. Why not try planning some activities each year for parents and teenagers to attend together? Mark DeVries presents this idea in his book, *Family-Based Youth Ministry*. He writes, "I began creating family-based youth ministry programs with one rule of thumb, if it works with teenagers, try it with youth and parents together."[140] Maybe he is on to something.

Resources

Finally, church leaders should do all they can to provide parents with some helpful resources and materials on parenting. These resources are plentiful today—check the Internet and your local Christian bookstore. Perhaps you could create a library of sorts within your ministry for parents to check out books, CDs, DVDs, or other practical resources to help them with their kids. You'll need to be discerning about what kind of materials you provide for them. You should read, listen, or watch everything first and only then make those resources available that you and your church would endorse or recommend.

As you gather resources for parents, don't forget the "people resources" that are a part of your church or community. What about doctors, police officers, child advocacy experts, lawyers, and counselors? Sometimes parents need these kinds of resources as well. Proverbs talks much about the *"multitude of counselors."*[141] It is my experience that a church can make some crucial contacts for parents when they are going through difficult times with their kids.

This four-prong strategy will encourage parents and will help get them on your side. We must not forget that the most effective youth ministry is undoubtedly a ministry that includes parents as a major focus.

"Train up a child in the way he should go,
And when he is old he will not depart from it."
Proverbs 22:6

Conversation #8
Stating the Obvious: What If There Are No Perfect Families or Churches Here?

Most people seem to like formulas in life. We want to know the outcome of a prescribed course of action; do something the way we are supposed to do it and everything will turn out the way we expect. Formulas work great in chemistry (for example, the molecular formula of aspirin is $C_9H_8O_4$), carpentry ("measure twice, cut once," for instance), and baking a cake (ask Betty Crocker). As creatures of habits, we want life to take a prescribed course. Many of us want that to be especially true with raising children: Do the right things and our kids will turn out fine. The problem is that life doesn't always work that way.

Parents and church leaders alike are particularly susceptible to this attitude. Perhaps this is because we look at verses like Proverbs 22:6, *"Train up a child in the way he should go, and when he is old he will not depart from it"* (which I also quoted above), as if it were a prescription or a pattern. But, as one author put it, "We misconstrue the Word of God when we treat proverbs as if they were divine promises."[142] That writer developed that thought more fully, adding, "Passages like these have been taken as indicating that Christian families experience blessings and loss from God, *quid pro quo*. We believe that God promises a wonderful family life to those who obey his commands."[143]

However, most of us realize that life doesn't always work out the way we intended. We can do what we think is right, with the proper motives, but sometimes things go wrong. In spite of good intentions, we all probably know Christian kids who grew up to not walk with God, and the horror stories that come from sinful choices can break our hearts. Some of us know people in our own families like this, and the pain for parents can be almost unmanageable. We want children to grow up and go on for God, but sometimes that doesn't happen the way we wanted.

Anyone who has been involved in youth ministry has undoubtedly also felt the disappointment of knowing teenagers who have walked away from God. This experience has happened with kids I know more than I want to admit. I can recall even now, numerous teens in whom I literally invested my life, time, and energy, only to have them make bad decisions to leave church, to hang out with negative friends, and to make sinful choices that ended up with serious consequences, sometimes with ruined lives. Even as I write this now, I am remembering their names and seeing their faces in my mind, and praying specifically for them to come back to God. Many of them were once actively involved in the youth groups I led and now they are not living for God, and it hurts deeply.

I absolutely believe in the authority, inerrancy, and inspiration of Scripture,[144] which also means that we should look at Biblical passages the way God intended, including specific verses in Proverbs. As I have emphasized over and over again in this book, Christian parents and church leaders must be intentional and must make Godly choices, and we must raise our kids with positive influences in their lives because we desperately want them to grow up to go on for God.

But raising kids isn't a formula—the process of growing up does not come with a guarantee.

So, in this chapter I am going to present a series of "what if" questions. This list represents real questions from real people who have struggled with real situations like these descriptions in the past or who are facing similar circumstances now. These questions are based on real stories. They are based on real life experiences with very real emotional responses.

I hasten to help readers understand that there are very seldom any easy answers in life. This list of questions will feature simple suggestions in reply, and it'd be natural for readers to come to the conclusion that life situations are easy to solve; certainly that's not the case. So please read this chapter, with my list of "what if" questions and the corresponding recommended action steps, with a heart of understanding realizing that my intent is to offer encouragement. I will propose ideas and suggestions for fellow-strugglers in this grand endeavor of helping the next generation to grow towards spiritual maturity.

Section for Christian Parents

All of us who are parents need to ask ourselves this critically important question—**what do we want for our kids?** Our answer will determine what specific action steps we take in the entire parenting process.

I certainly understand that most parents want their kids to grow up to be happy and successful. But, I'll keep saying this over and over again, as a believer in the Lord Jesus Christ and as someone who has a lifetime desire to serve Him, I would much rather have my kids grow up to be Godly than successful; and I would much rather they live holy lives, than seek happiness[145] in what the world has to offer.

1. <u>**What if your children do not want to make the things of the Lord a priority**</u>? Answers in Genesis author and speaker, Ken Ham writes, "Only 11 percent of those who have left the Church were still attending [church] during the college years. Almost 90 percent of them were lost in middle school and high school. By the time they got to college they were already gone! About 40 percent are leaving the Church during elementary and middle school years!"[146] According to Ham's book, *Already Gone* (with Christian researcher, Britt Beemer), somewhere

around 60 to 70 percent of Christian kids who once participated in Sunday School and youth group will quit active involvement in the church, and many of them will actually leave during middle school or high school. His premise is this—they are "Already Gone!"

My wife and I have met so many discouraged parents in our travels who are facing this exact situation with their kids. At one point their children loved attending church and church functions. Their friends were there and they enjoyed the activities and gatherings. They had good relationships with their adult teachers and seemed to be on track toward continued active involvement in church and church events. Then something happened that changed their point of view.

We should be honest enough here to admit that puberty itself is enough to change a young person's emotional, physical, and mental outlook.[147] Wise parents certainly need to research the important topic of childhood and adolescent development to help their children transition through the often difficult world of today's adolescence. Since reading Ham's book (mentioned above), I began to look into his assertion that actually many of today's Christian young people begin to check out of church, either physically, emotionally, or spiritually, way before they graduate from high school. I had specific conversations with several parents and teenagers that were facing the same circumstances.

In many cases, he was correct. Here is a list of some of the reasons I heard, in no real priority order, about why kids would want to leave church and youth group:
- I don't have any friends there.
- The teacher/leader said or did something that was discouraging.
- The people there are too judgmental.
- The church is too legalistic.

- They don't teach the Bible so that I can understand it.
- It's boring.
- There are too many cliques.
- I'm too busy with school activities, homework, and my job.
- The people there are hypocrites.
- I want to try something else.
- I just don't like it.

So, what can parents do when they notice their children begin to become more and more disinterested in church? Here are a few things to think through: (1) <u>Talk to your children</u> specifically, lovingly, and intentionally to see if they are really born again. 1 John 3:14-16 indicates that true Christ followers will want fellowship with God's people. Parents, I don't want to offend anyone here, but are you sure that your kids are truly saved? (2) <u>Make church and church functions a priority anyway</u>. As I have already mentioned, I came to Christ as a young boy and grew up in a home that made church and church functions at top priority; but I'm sure there were times when I was a pre-teen or teenager when I didn't really want to attend church or youth group. My parents made me go anyway. I am not advocating that parents should turn church attendance into a huge fight, but I am saying I believe it should be a top priority. Strong Christian parents should make attending church a vital part of the family culture: It is a habit—it's just what we do as a family. (3) <u>Pray consistently and fervently for them</u>. Don't forget that this is definitely a matter to take before the Lord. He can change things! (4) <u>Look in a mirror</u>. Are you faithfully committed to church yourself, or have you been critical and negative about church or church leaders in front of your kids? If so, ask them for forgiveness and show them you are going to change. Parents, you will do your children a huge favor by verbally and intentionally making church a priority. (5) <u>Do you have unrealistic</u>

expectations for your children? I've met many, many parents who want their children to grow up to be successful athletes, scholars, musicians, or business executives. Or they just want their children to do something to make a lot of money. Those things are fine in themselves, but perhaps parents are unwittingly putting undue pressure on their kids. I'd rather see my children grow up to love the Lord, to live faithfully for Him, and to serve Him with their entire lives!

2. **What if your children do not grow up to live for the Lord?** The accounts are numerous of young people who grew up in church and seemed to have great potential for on-going spiritual success, but for whatever reason landed in crash-and-burn situations. Their bad decisions and sinful choices led to disaster after disaster or a slow fade into sinful behavior, and their parents, other family members, and even church leaders felt exasperated and dismayed.

There are other stories just as prevalent of young adults who once seemed to be on a course toward spiritual success, but who just decided to leave the church. Their lives featured personal and/or career choices that did not prioritize the Lord or His work, and instead focused on success, wealth, or human achievement.

Both groups generated confusion and frustration in the hearts of their parents.

So, what are Christian parents to do if their children decide to leave the church after high school? Here are some simple ideas: (1) Remember, the end of their story is not written yet. Parents in this situation should understand that there is still time, and there is always hope. Trust the Lord with your kids. The "Prodigal Son" story in Luke 15:11-32 can be a source of encouragement to you. The younger son went through some very difficult times, and your kids may go through some bumps along the way too. But in the end of that story, the Prodigal came back. God can certainly make that happen in your family as well. I went through some of those bumps in my life as a high schooler too. I'm very thankful my parents didn't write me off, but kept encouraging me and praying for me during those days. (2) Pray for them fervently and constantly. We serve a big God, Who is in the business of bringing people to Himself. He can do this for your kids too. (3) Continue to live consistently before the Lord and follow His will. Your faithful example will shine incredibly bright in their lives. Enough said. (4) Seek advice, counsel, and encouragement from other Christian parents who can offer Godly help during these days of transition. As we talked about in Conversation #7, we need "Titus 2 churches" where older parents can and will mentor and encourage younger parents. There are probably spiritually mature people like that in your church. Swallow your pride about your kids and go talk with them, and at least get them praying for you and your kids. Then prayerfully consider listening to and heeding their advice. (5) Love your children. You don't need to condone their lifestyle or overlook any sinful habits that may be in their lives. But, love them in the Lord and let them know you love them. This will help more than you know.

3. **What if the local church is not all that it should be?** The following phrase has been around for years, and I have seen it to be attributed to great contemporary preachers like Billy Graham and Chuck Swindoll, "If you find the perfect church, don't join it because you will ruin it." But, as I dug a little further I found this statement that is actually rooted in a quotation from Charles Haddon Spurgeon:

> You that are members of the church have not found it perfect and I hope that you feel almost

glad that you have not. If I had never joined a Church till I had found one that was perfect, I should never have joined one at all! And the moment I did join it, if I had found one, I should have spoiled it, for it would not have been a perfect Church after I had become a member of it. Still, imperfect as it is, it is the dearest place on earth to us...The Church is faulty, but that is no excuse for your not joining it, if you are the Lord's. Nor need your own faults keep you back, for the Church is not an institution for perfect people, but a sanctuary for sinners saved by Grace, who, though they are saved, are still sinners and need all the help they can derive from the sympathy and guidance of their fellow Believers. [148]

I wholeheartedly agree. Parents, your local church may never be all that you want it to be. But, Biblically-speaking, the church is still God's work, and it is what God is using to accomplish His work in the world today. [149]

We must never trivialize the work of God by making other things more important, like community soccer leagues, homework, or a job to save money for college. It's a mistake to teach our children to commit to something else, and then not demonstrate a personal and family commitment to the local church. As I've mentioned elsewhere in this book, our kids tend to see God as unimportant if we don't make His work a top priority.

We also should not ignore the church because we see its many weaknesses. Emerging generations are likely on their own to grow up with a sense of idealism that tends to pinpoint their own flaws in the church. Authors Kevin

DeYoung and Ted Kluck[150] made a compilation of some of these perceived liabilities as identified recently by young adults. Here are a few that made their list, and a few others I added from my conversations with families:

- The church doesn't understand the community.
- The church has poor leadership.
- The church is run like a business.
- The church has no vision.
- The church is graying quickly.
- The church is inbred.
- The church is out of touch.
- The church is all about money.
- The church is too political.
- The church is judgmental and negative.
- The church is dominated by males and is oppressive to females.
- The church is homophobic.
- The church is obsessed with evangelism.
- The church is too sheltered.
- The church is unhelpful toward the disabled.
- The church does not support single moms.
- The church is too shallow.
- The church is too theological.
- The church is unfriendly.
- The church overlooks singles.
- The church is not evangelistic enough.
- The church seems like a concert.
- The church does not take a stand.
- And so on...

The local church dominated the lives of early Christ-followers (see passages like Acts 2:24; Acts 11:21-26; 1 Corinthians 11:18; 1 Corinthians 12-14; 1 Corinthians 16:2; Philippians 4:15; 1 Timothy 4:13; and Hebrew 10:25). To them, the church meant things like mission, teaching, worship, service, fellowship, and community. That's why it is so essential for Christian parents to build involvement in the local church as a top priority into the lives of the next generation.

Here then is some practical advice for parents[151] and other family members if you think your church is struggling in some important areas: (1) <u>Pray much</u>—the church is God's work, and He can surely work; (2) <u>Search the Scriptures</u> to make sure your beliefs are actually Biblical, and especially participate in the church events that preach and teach the Bible; (3) <u>Talk to your pastor, the elders, or other church leaders and express your sincere concerns with them</u>. Do not gossip, and do not become a negative influence by criticizing the church to others that have nothing to do with the solution; (4) <u>Get involved in something through the church</u>— remember it's not about you; the church must be about Christ, so find some place there where you can use your gifts and abilities to serve Him.

I have one final suggestion here for parents: <u>Don't make excuses for not being active in the church, or for not encouraging your children to get involved in church</u>. I understand the human reasons for not wanting to go to church could be numerous—for example, the youth group has carnal teens, there's not many teenagers in this church, Sunday morning is the only family time we have, there is no young adult group or no singles group in this church, or innumerable other excuses. We must understand that participation in church is not just because of its benefit to us or to our families. It must be because we love the Lord, want to grow in Him, desire to serve Him, follow His commands, and want to be a part of what He is doing.

Section for Church Leaders

Pastors, youth workers, and other church leaders: Before we launch into some possible answers to the questions I have listed below, let's take a few moments to revisit a very important topic I briefly mentioned in Conversation #6 and then again in Conversation #8. This discussion may actually require a ministry-changing, direction-altering decision from all of us. It's that important! We desperately need to have this conversation, and then purposefully think though the ramifications of what we are talking about. I'm talking about a wrong perception so many of today's church leaders, especially, perhaps, youth pastors and other youth workers, have of parents of the children and youth in our ministries. I've heard so many pastors, youth pastors, and other church leaders criticize parents and families.

To be honest, I've met a ton of youth workers who look at parents of the kids in their groups like they are almost the enemy. The parents are the ones who keep teens from attending youth group. The parents schedule or allow conflicting activities. The parents don't make the right decisions to ensure that youth ministry activities or church functions are at the top of the family's priority list. I referred to the lengthy conversation I had with a fairly large group of youth pastors and lay youth workers earlier who indicated that the parents of teenagers in their groups were their greatest concern.

If you are a youth worker or other church leader who looks at parents that way, I want to take this opportunity to bluntly, but lovingly confront you about that attitude. Please don't feel that way! Throughout this book, I have made some very serious challenges to parents about the importance of raising kids to go on for God. I have spoken over and over again about family priorities and the significance of the local church. But I need to go on record here as saying this: **It's not necessarily their job to support you**! Nor is it their greatest concern that your meeting, function, or activity is well attended.

Believe me, I've been where you are. I have known several parents who made the wrong choices for their kids, and I have worked with many, many families who chose to do other things instead of attending my youth group meetings or scheduled church functions. In many cases I had personal conversations with those parents—and several of those talks did not end very well. Parents seem to take things very personally when someone points out something they may be doing incorrectly with their families. But over the years, I learned that some Christian parents really wanted to do the right thing and actually did want their kids to grow into spiritual maturity. They just went about it differently than I thought they should.

So throughout this entire process, please remember that **it is your job to support them;** and as you do that, they are more likely to show their support of the church! Parents have huge responsibilities in raising their kids, and they need all the support they can get from the church, which includes the greater community of Christ-followers and especially includes the mentoring relationships and help that comes from older parents who have already gone through this process with their own kids. Pastors and other church leaders must look at parents as allies, not as enemies. We're doing the same things and we're on the same side—encouraging (teaching, training, and equipping) the next generation to grow up and go on for God.

What if parents are not very supportive of your church's programs?

So what should church leaders do if parents and their families are not committed to church programs like youth group, Sunday services, and other regular functions? We've already discussed how this is likely to be a situation that many pastors and youth pastors will face today. I get it that the solutions are never as easy as this sounds, but here are a few things to think through:

1. Remember, <u>it is possible that a parent **may** be making the correct choice if their student does not attend</u> youth group meetings or other church functions. For instance, it has been my experience that high-achieving kids (in academics, athletics, or other extracurricular activities for example) or students in families with very real financial needs will probably be very busy working or involved in their corresponding activities. Involvements like this can be very legitimate and even necessary. It is also very possible that families actually do have other

matters on their schedules. (See the *I Want Busy Kids in Our Student Ministry* article in Appendix 3.) Like I've pointed out above, maybe just a simple conversation with the parents will help you see things from their perspective.

2. Also remember, <u>you do not know everything that is going on in their family</u>. Please appreciate the reality that today's parents are facing unbelievable pressures from both internal and external influences. Raising kids in this environment is hard. It has been my experience that some parents make choices you and I might not make, but we must understand that we are not in that specific situation, and we are not walking in their shoes.

    If your church offers parenting classes, this can be a good time to talk about the importance and philosophy behind your church's meetings and events in a less threatening, group-like setting. The importance of Biblically-based parental choices is one reason I am such a strong advocate for a training and equipping ministry for parents, especially those parents of pre-teens and teenagers. Classes like this can help parents understand why it is so significant for the families and their young people to attend those functions. You can also make resources available at this time to assist parents with their decision making, and possibly provide a forum there for older parents to have a voice of encouragement to the young parents in your church.

3. <u>Be sensitive to family and community schedules</u>. I personally struggle with another attitude that seems to be somewhat prevalent among youth workers and other church leaders today. Too many pastors plan church events and ministries that fit their own personal timetables without taking the needs or

schedules of families into account. Or churches will host functions on a specific night of the week or at a set time because it has "always been" held then, also without taking into consideration the current needs and rhythm of the community or area around them.

I'll list a couple of fictional examples to help make my point:

- Youth Pastor Chad sets the schedule for his discipleship group to meet on Tuesday evenings because that's the night that works best for his family; but the local public school's basketball games are usually held on Tuesdays, which means those athletes can't attend the meetings.

- First Community Church has held youth group on Sunday evenings for several decades, so the church elders think that is the best time for the meetings to be held. But it is harder and harder for parents to carve out time on Sundays due to their kids' homework, sports events, and work schedules.

It is so important for churches today to be sensitive to the surrounding culture. That includes the basic schedule of the general community, like the time most residents go to work in the mornings and the time they return home, the school calendar, and the timetable for community, schools, and family-oriented activities. An awareness of these community rhythms will give the church a renewed credibility with families and will prove to be a benefit both for regular church attendees and for evangelistic outreach. It might be time for your church to reevaluate when to hold classes, services, meetings, and events to better minister to the current needs of families.

I beg church leaders to give this some prayerful thought. Is your programming based on your own schedule, or the way things have always been done? Or can your church creatively plan and hold events when it makes the most sense for the community and culture?

4. <u>Commit to reach and disciple young people—even if they don't always show up for your program</u>. Since I have been somewhat direct already in this chapter, I will continue here in that vein. Let me remind readers that I absolutely love local church youth workers and have dedicated my life's ministry to champion church youth ministry. But we need to change the attitude that says the effective ministry means, "come to my program." Then we respond in frustration if, for whatever the reason, they don't come. I believe it's time to shatter that paradigm.

Let's remember that God's "Great Commission" in Matthew 28:19-20 begins with the injunction to "go." Let's take that to heart. Instead of a stance that says to teenagers, "attend my events and I'll minister to you," maybe the answer is that we reach them by going to them. In other words, if churches are really serious about reaching and discipling teenagers, we'll commit to do whatever it takes to make that happen. It might mean hosting some teenagers in your home for Bible studies around the kitchen table, or meeting high school athletes for early morning prayer in a local coffee shop or fast food restaurant. Youth workers and other church leaders who are serious about reaching kids can show up for *their* school plays, concerts, or athletic events, or can volunteer for involvement in a local school as a way to reach out to other teenagers. Please, don't assume your ministry with teenagers is done if they don't come to your events. There are other ways to impact them, if we are willing to do what it takes.

5. <u>Don't waste their time in your programming</u>. There is one other observation I've made during my visits to churches that keeps some parents and high-achieving teens from wanting to be a part of your events. If they feel as if what you are doing there is not important, they are not going to attend. This is why it is so important that church leaders effectively communicate in every way possible the clear purpose of these meetings or events. Believe me, if you don't know why kids should come, then they won't either, and probably will not attend.
Here are some other important questions in considering the importance of your church functions:
    *   Are you adequately prepared?
    *   Is your meeting space ready to go, and is it set up properly for what you are trying to accomplish?
    *   Do you start on time?
    *   Do you use the allotted time effectively?

I don't want to offend anyone here, but I have been in so many youth meetings that did not start on time, and where it was obvious the leader was not really prepared. I will admit that there have been times when I've had to "wing it" as well; but friends, this should be the rare exception, not the norm. The ongoing spiritual lives of our young people are too important.

I've also been in several youth gatherings recently where the leader leaves several minutes at the start of the program for the attendees to fellowship or just "hang out" with each other. That's fine, and in some cases it may be quite beneficial. But let me give you some advice—if you do that, make sure your group and their parents know why. You don't want people in your church to think you are just "killing time."

Here's what Dan Koller had to say in a recent blog from *Youth Specialties*: "This generation isn't one to sit on the sidelines. They want to get their hands dirty." He warns, "When our ministries lack a true missional purpose, students will disengage. They want to be a part of something bigger than themselves. They want to help build, shape, and carry out the mission. If we are honest, most of our ministries have a mission statement, but in reality, we don't pursue that mission. This generation doesn't want a slogan to chant, they want a mission to live."[152]

What if Christian parents in your church willfully decide not to involve their children in the church youth or children's activities?

This is another issue I need to briefly address. In my travels to churches, I have met some Christian parents who make a deliberate decision not to allow their teenagers to attend church functions. It may be, as I mentioned elsewhere in this book, that they believe they are the only ones who can and should have a spiritual impact on their kids. They also may think that other teenagers might be carnal and have a negative influence, so the parents decide not to involve their young people.

As I stated in Conversation #3, I believe this is an arrogant attitude and I will go on record here as saying it is a mistake. Christian parents must understand their kids need the church. They need the influence of Godly adults in their lives, they need to be a part of the larger Christian community, and they need the fellowship of other Christian peers.

I admit I am not a fan of the phrase that I have heard recently from several speakers and writers on the subject of Christian parents and the church—that "parents are to be the primary disciplers of their children."[153] I understand their point, and I see the validity and importance of passages like Deuteronomy 6, Deuteronomy 11, Psalm 78:1-8, and Ephesians

6:1-4. But, I see in Scripture that real concept of "discipleship" (which is mentioned close to 300 times in the New Testament[154]) is not in actuality a command to parents, but instead is used as a call to follow Christ[155] wholeheartedly. It was a specific training and teaching method of students learning by intentionally[156] following a teacher around in a variety of real-life learning experiences. In other words, discipleship in Scripture was life-on-life training by a qualified teacher or rabbi—someone other than the student's parent. Of course practically speaking, parents may have this role in their child's life for a while, but eventually, we see biblically that discipleship means learning from others as well.

Another reason parents keep their kids from church is the concern that other teenagers in the group present a carnal and harmful presence. If that is actually the case, should parents keep their kids away from the church's youth ministry? But if it is true there are troubled kids who are struggling in the youth group, then even more so, that group needs the positive and spiritual influence of strong, Godly kids who may be a catalyst for real change in the group. I have witnessed that happening many, many times in my own experience in youth ministry. There can be an opportunity there for mature Christian young people to have a positive influence on the rest of the group. Certainly, this is a conversation worth having, both with the parents and then with the students from those families. Obviously this matter should be handled with the proverbial "kids gloves." It has been my experience that the parents who feel this way often do so with firm opinions. For the sake of unity in the church and in the youth group, it might be wise to involve older, mature believers in the conversation. Perhaps that could be the church's lead pastor, older Godly parents, or even an outside voice.

I'm just not convinced that the solution for parents is to keep their kids out of the youth group. Of course there are other viewpoints out there, but church leaders should have a mature and Biblically-based conversation with these parents, with the motive being that all parties are totally committed to the ongoing spiritual success of the family and for the kids to mature spiritually.

What if parents in your church are not living consistent Christian lives?

This is something that can be a significant hindrance to our objective of helping young people grow up and go on for God, and that is when "Christian" parents are living inconsistent, carnal, and sinful lives. The research is very clear—if our students grow up in a consistent Christian home and have the support of a reinforcing, Bible-teaching church, they are the ones most likely to grow towards spiritual maturity.[157] According to LifeWay Research, "Teens who have parents who are authentic examples of Christian faith—proactive and consistent in living out their faith—also are more likely to keep attending as young adults. Across the board, 20 percent more of those who stayed indicated they had parents or family members who discussed spiritual things, gave them spiritual guidance and prayed together."[158] It's very clear: When these two God-given institutions (the church and the family) provide a consistent message and philosophy for encouraging kids toward spiritual maturity, kids are much more likely to live for God and be involved in His work for the rest of their lives.

Of course, there is also an individual, personal responsibility for people to grow spiritually,[159] and I'm not saying it is impossible for kids to go on for God if they are from families that are weak spiritually. God's grace is indeed *amazing*, and we've all seen the Lord do great things in and through the lives of young people who grew up with inconsistent parents.

The truth remains—many of these kids are growing up with obviously inconsistent, even hypocritical parents, and that's tough to overcome. But in God's grace He has given you the great privilege of having the opportunity to change that scenario. That's why true discipleship is so powerful. An unrelated, outside-the-family adult can build a growing, healthy relationship with these students and can truly have a lasting impact.

It's so important to pray specifically and fervently for these kids, and search the Scriptures for counsel and applicable principles to share with the students. Youth leaders will also need to carve out the time in their own schedules to personally interact with them with the goal of showing them it is possible to live a consistent Christian life. Again, I am always encouraged by passages, like 2 Timothy 3:10-17, that vividly gives us the account of how Paul discipled Timothy, who as I wrote about earlier, was himself from a dysfunctional family.[160]

It will be important for the church leaders to be sensitive to the parents, remembering that Dad and Mom, or even a legal guardian, have the final authority over the kids. This, of course, presents a dilemma because you want what's best for the kids, and you see the inconsistency in their family. We must never discount the resources God has provided for His people, like His Word, prayer, and the overall body of Christ—we always have those "weapons" at our disposal.

This is another "what if" situation that will demand effective and regular communication from the church to the parents. Even though you see the obvious weaknesses in the lives of the parents, communication is a must. Tell them often what you are doing and why. And do everything you can in an attempt to minister to them.

Stay encouraged. Situations like this that make youth ministry so important. God can use you as you stay close to Him and stay faithful to His call to reach the next generation.

What if there are young people from non-Christian families who attend your church?

A quick review of the history of youth ministry[161] will reveal a long line of visionary leaders who saw the reality of a growing youth culture and grasped the necessity of reaching teenagers with the Gospel. It's true that evangelism is at the very heart of contemporary youth ministry. However, as time has progressed, many church-based youth ministries have focused on the kids they already have, the sons and daughters of regular church attendees, instead of making the commitment in programming and relational efforts to reach kids for Christ.[162] I am not saying this as a critic, but to remind church leaders of the importance of reaching out to the unsaved teenagers in your communities. We need to remember that most people accept Christ when they are young.[163] There are hurdles in today's growing secular and postmodern culture to be sure, but it is also very possible for church leaders to make reaching kids for Christ a top emphasis in their programming efforts.[164]

In other words, this is the bottom line—if you are reaching kids for Christ, you will undoubtedly have young people from unsaved families in your youth group. Here are some quick, practical suggestions then for trying to reach out to those parents: (1) As I have said over and over again in this chapter, church leaders must stay sensitive to the parents—this is so important, even for unsaved parents. Please remember they still have the authority over the kids and may have strong concerns about why church people would have any interest in their children. (2) Make it a priority to communicate to them and get to know them. Be creative and be persistent. Find ways to get information about your church and your program into their hands. (3) Make the kids' safety a primary concern. Most parents, no matter what their spiritual condition, will be concerned about their children's safety. Make sure your church's child protection policy is in place and is enforced, and make sure to communicate to them all you are doing to keep kids safe as they participate in your ministry. (4) Pray often for them and for the kids from these families. Never underestimate the importance of prayer. Have your leadership team pray fervently and consistently for the other family members to come to Christ. Maybe He will use you and your ministry to reach new families for Christ. (5) That brings me to my next suggestion, present the Gospel. It is the Word of God that changes peoples' lives. The world can do youth programming, but only Christ's church has the message of eternal life. (6) Look for ways to integrate kids from these families into the overall life of the church. There are lots of ways to accomplish this—for example: mentoring, a "big brother/big sister" approach, etc. Almost any way that you can "adopt" kids from weak families into strong families is a good idea.

There are no perfect families and there are no perfect churches. However, both institutions are designed by God to be catalysts for the long-term spiritual growth and maturity of our kids. The process of encouraging the next generation to grow up and go on for God will certainly have its ups and downs with some successes and some heartbreaks. It's so important for Christian parents and church leaders to remember that we're in this journey together.

We'll discuss more about how the church can be *a family* for the long-term benefit of kids in the next conversation.

*"...having predestined us to **adoption as sons** by Jesus Christ to Himself, according to the good pleasure of His will."*
Ephesians 1:5

Conversation #9
It Takes a Church: How Can the Church be a Family, In a "Family-Unfriendly" Culture?

The Scriptures include a series of interesting metaphors[165] about the church that provide vivid and practical pictures of how God's church is supposed to function. These illustrations help us to see the church in tangible and real-life ways. Four of these Biblical descriptions relate specifically to marriage, families, parents, and children—the church is the "bride of Christ,"[166] the church is the "body of Christ,"[167] the church is "God's house,"[168] and the main one that I want to focus on, the church is "the *family* or household of God."[169]

In addition to these comparisons, the Bible also provides us with another concept of family when He uses the idea of "adoption"[170] as an apt illustration of our relationship with the Heavenly Father, through His Son, Jesus Christ.[171] It's thrilling to realize that God Himself adopts us into His family. According to author Trevor Burke, "Adoption graphically and intimately describes the family character of Christianity, and is a basic description...of what it means to be a Christian."[172]

It's obvious from God's Word that the Lord wants His church to be a family, and to operate like a family. Yet, today's church is too often operated like a business, an institution, a social club, or a youth rally, instead of a family.

It's time for the church to throw away the organizational flow charts and entertainment-driven programming in favor of being a family—loving, welcoming, including, accepting, forgiving, challenging, confronting, disciplining, motivating, teaching, and modeling. The family metaphor fits perfectly with the premise of this book. Parents have offspring—children who grow up and reproduce—and the family continues.

Do you remember the important passage I discussed in Conversation #6 with the great illustration of real-life mentoring that is presented to us in Acts 11:19-26? Barnabas and Saul (not yet called Paul[173]) spent a year in Antioch encouraging and teaching the new believers who were a part of that early church. At the end of their time there, we are told *"the disciples were first called Christians in Antioch."* There is some indication from the text that this was actually a derogatory term—essentially a put down. The end result of the ministry of these two church leaders was that the people there were pointed to Christ. I mentioned before that they didn't become "little Barnabas'" or "little Saul"; instead they were obviously Christians, or "little Christs." They were a part of the family, so much so that they took on the characteristics and nature of Jesus Christ. That is exactly what our ministries today should be all about. We too must point people to Jesus. They need to see Jesus when they show up at our churches, and then be actively welcomed into the family of believers gathered there.

There should be a loving unity that is much more than the old *Cheers* TV show theme song:

> *Making your way in the world today, takes everything you've got;*
> *Taking a break from all your worries, sure would help a lot.*
> *Wouldn't you like to get away?*
> *Sometimes you want to go, where everybody knows your name, and*
> *they're always glad you came;*
> *You want to be where you can see, our troubles are all the same;*

You want to be where everybody knows your name.[174]

Even if it's just a song from a TV show, many people have come to believe they'd like to be a part of a place like that—a place "where everybody knows your name."

People are always looking for community. As one youth ministry specialist put it, "As much as faith in Jesus is about a 'personal relationship,' it can only be worked out in community. And community only happens with students through a safe environment that is an authentic, consistent time together, building memories, and spurring one another on toward love and good deeds!"[175]

It may seem ironic in today's "family unfriendly"[176] culture, but it has been my experience that most people would love to be a part of an authentic community where the people are loving and accepting and committed to the personal growth and maturity of each person. I don't need to recite the statistics here, but in a culture where the definition of marriage is changing at warp speed, with more and more adult singles, and with a mounting number of non-traditional family situations, people will crave the family environment that a true local church can provide.

In the cases of strong Christian families, the genuine partnership and collaboration between Christian parents and the church is essential.[177] But in many, many situations today (and the trend away from solid families is exploding), the church must "be a family," and must act as a community for effective outreach and ministry in today's "family unfriendly" world.

How Can the Church Act Like a Family in Today's Culture?

Friends, if you know me or have followed my ministry, you know I love the family. I love *my family*—from my parents, to my brothers, to my wife, our children, and our grandchildren, to my extended family. (We probably should all appear on an episode of "Dr. Phil" or with some other television psychoanalyst because we are all so strange; but they are my family and I love them dearly.) And, I love *the family*. I have taught family ministry courses in two different Christian colleges for over 15 years. Plus, my wife and I have led marriage, parenting, and family ministry conferences in churches all around the country for quite a few years.

I also love *the church* and have dedicated my life to serving the Lord in and through His church. I appreciate creative church ministries, and I love visiting churches (of all sizes, by the way) that are being strategic and intentional about reaching out to the culture around them.

But please hear me out. Churches that minister exclusively to strong Christian families are not fulfilling the Biblical purpose for the church. The trend is actually headed in the opposite direction, and the church must be prepared to reach out to a culture where the family unit is seriously in trouble and where Godly parents are a shrinking minority. Of course I firmly believe that strong families still desperately need the church, even those families that are led by Godly parents who love the Lord and who are doing their best to raise their children to love Him and serve Him. And the church certainly needs families like I just described that are supportive of the work God is doing there. Of course, pastors, elders, and other church leaders should be totally committed to equipping today's parents to be spiritual leaders in their homes and to help them to be spiritual successes with their children. But that is not the norm today, nor is culture likely to head back to being "family friendly"[178] any time soon.

By using the term "family friendly," I am not promoting the idea of a church that is geared toward good, normal, or traditional families only. Neither am I saying that churches should only minister to the parents who appear to be strong Christians with their parenting-act together. My experience teaches me that those people (the ones who act like they have a nice, normal, and spiritually-oriented family) will be, as my dad used to say, "a dime a dozen." The pervasive Christian culture in today's churches has seemingly created an environment where it is easy to put on a "successful Christian" mask that hides the truth about what may be really going on in the home.

My wife and I have tried to develop an attitude that hopefully accepts assistance, advice, and training from anyone that can help us with our family, instead of hiding our struggles in some misguided sense of pride that masks the truth to fellow believers. There is way too much of that in most churches today. Plus, I'm not entirely sure that the "good Christian family" actually exists very much anymore. Readers assuredly know what I mean.

I use this term here to indicate that there must be two clear priorities for church programming and scheduling. One, we must be sensitive to all kinds of families—the growing number of households that would be considered as non-traditional families, AND to those of our congregants who represent strong, Godly families, plus all of the homes that fall somewhere in the middle. And two, we should be building churches that will be *a family* to the growing number of people in our communities who are without solid, affirming, and supportive family situations. I think it benefits church leaders to lead their churches in an intentional strategic planning process that includes all ministries of the church with the goal of moving your entire church toward a family-friendly approach. This plan will unquestionably become increasingly important as time goes on.

The strategy to move a church in this direction should include:

- Leadership – If this approach is a new direction for your church, it will be imperative to get your church's leadership on board before you begin to change the course. Communication will be the key to help the leaders understand the reasons for this adjustment in philosophy. So do not ignore this basic first step. Help them understand the Biblical basis for the church operating as a family, and show them the demographic trends in your area that show how many potential households there that would be considered non-traditional.

- <u>Preaching & Teaching</u> – The next step is to share the Biblical basis for this philosophical move by preaching on it from the pulpit and by teaching your people why it is so important for the church to think this way. I hope that some of the passages presented and discussed in this book could become the foundation for what to share with your people.

- <u>Children's Ministry</u> – A "family-friendly" church begins with the children's department staff members. They must be an integral part of the vision to connect with both Christian and unsaved, unchurched households. This absolutely means that your church's ministry to children provides a safe setting with qualified, trained, prepared, and loving children's workers who are knowledgeable and creative communicators of Biblical truth that relates to the lives of the specific age groups of the children attending. It also means that the children's classes are welcoming and inviting to the children from your community who may be from non-traditional family situations. As mentioned earlier, this situation will be more and more likely in today's culture.

- <u>Youth Ministry</u> – Youth ministry is also a key element in reaching out to today's culture. In fact, this aspect of your church's overall ministry may be more important now than ever before. I have been actively involved in youth ministry in a variety of different roles for over 40 years. Plus, I have been a lifelong student of youth ministry and have studied and read extensively on the history of youth ministry in the United States. My office walls are lined with almost every youth ministry book that has been published in the last four decades. Yep, I am definitely a youth ministry insider—and yet, I believe that in many circles youth ministry is being deemphasized or downplayed as never before. I think this is also a mistake. Each individual local church will need to determine where to allocate its staffing budget, but I still believe in the calling and training of youth pastors. Parents of teenagers are much more likely to attend and actively participate in a local church that has invested much in ministries and programs for their kids. Most communities in this country are dominated by a prevailing youth culture that provides enough incentive for churches to utilize their youth ministry as a strategic part of their outreach endeavors.

- Inter-Generational Family Ministries – As I have highlighted throughout this book, inter-generational connections are indispensable for churches that are truly interested in operating like a family. We must return to the "Titus 2 imperative" we discussed earlier, where Godly older people build growing personal relationships with younger adults in the church to help them and their families with specific matters, such as marriage and raising children. I believe in a balance of course, but churches should quit separating adults by age groups only and instead develop practical ways to connect the generations.

- Worship Services – In most churches perhaps, the main worship service has become the focal point of entry for visitors to the church. This makes these services of utmost importance for a "family-friendly" philosophy. The seating arrangement, the music used, the message, and especially the ushers and greeters should all be positioned and utilized to welcome guests from the community. In some of the churches I visited, guests were publicly identified with some attempt to glean personal contact information from them for follow-up purposes. Other churches treated visitors almost anonymously, not trying to call attention to them in any way. The approaches varied, but churches will need to determine which method works best in their area. The important thing is to remember that we are living in a post-church[179] and post-Christian[180] culture that demands a missional approach from churches. The people who most often visit your church are likely to do so only by personal invitation from a current member. According to a recent article in *Christianity Today*, "The personal invitation is an effective way to break down any real or perceived barriers one might have to walking into a new church building or being willing to engage in a new circle of people."[181] And church visitors in today's post-church culture are quite likely to be from an unchurched or non-religious background and may feel somewhat threatened by the "religious practices" habitually found in so many churches.[182] Even though the real purpose of church worship services is to utilize music as a public means of worshipping the Lord and to prepare the hearts of people to hear the message from God's Word, it is still very important to remember that these services will likely be the occasion when most visitors show up to check out the church. That's why the worship services should also be positioned and organized to greet, welcome, and accept guests into the church.

- <u>Mentoring Ministries</u> – The actual family unit provides a great generation-to-generation illustration of how mentoring works: grandparents teach parents who teach children. This progression makes perfect sense. Older women teach the younger women, and older men teach the younger men. It works in teaching people how to make quilts, how to fix the Thanksgiving turkey, how to play the piano, how to repair the family car, and in how to run the family farm. It also works in the Christian life in church ministry—and that's the beauty and practicality of Titus 2:1-8. One of the most practical ways for a church to act like a family is for it to provide generation-to-generation mentoring relationships.

- <u>Counseling Ministries</u> – There's one other potential ministry opportunity that can be especially beneficial for churches ministering in today's secular and sin-saturated culture, and that is the ministry of counseling. Let's face it, so many people today are struggling through personal life decisions that have caused havoc in their lives, in their marriages, or in the lives of their children. There undoubtedly will be multiple occasions to assist and equip people who may have some connection with your church via counseling. Of course, your church will need to explore the legal qualifications and specific guidelines that may be present in your state or even within your church's denomination before hanging out a "shingle" indicating there is a counselor present. Your church should also do some homework before launching such a ministry and will need to answer some specific questions that relate to this decision. (For instance: who will do the counseling? Should a woman only counsel other women? What specific approach or philosophy of counseling should you embrace?) But, believe me, if your church is serious about reaching out to the unsaved and unchurched households in your community, you will have plenty of counseling opportunities to handle.

Ministering to "Spiritual Orphans"

With the goal of helping the next generation grow up and go on for God in mind and if you are serious about reaching out to your community, there will unquestionably be the people I call "spiritual orphans" who will need to be included in your church's plan and approach to ministry. Spiritual orphans are individuals who have come to Christ, but who do not have the spiritual support system in place to grow in Him. I am not talking here about orphans in their relationship with Christ. If they have put their faith in Christ, then indeed they have been adopted into God's family and have been brought out of their sin and into a new life in Christ. But some people who have been saved have difficulty finding a place in the body of Christ and forming relationships with fellow believers who can help them grow. I've met spiritual orphans of all ages, but for the sake of our discussion here, let's talk specifically about young people.

If your church has an effective youth ministry, you are probably seeing young people accept Christ through their interaction with some of your regular kids or through their participation in one of your outreach-oriented youth events. Praise the Lord! It's always a blessing to see members of the next generation make personal commitments for Christ.

As I've mentioned already, the discipline and practice of youth ministry came into fruition with the desire to reach teenagers for Christ.[183] That's why parachurch youth ministry organizations got started and that's why many churches originally hired professional youth workers.

However, I'm wondering now if churches are doing all we can to reach out to these new Christians with an effort to assimilate them into the family of God and into the larger community of faith in the local church. I'm not sure that this practice, helping to fold new believers into the church, is something most churches are very good at doing. In fact, government and community programs may be better at this idea than the church. We've all heard of initiatives like "foster parents"[184] and "big brother and big sister"[185] programs. These organizations work hard to reach out to young people that need the influence of significant older adults in their lives.

One idea that has worked successfully in several churches I visited was for some of the parents of active teenagers in the youth group to "adopt" their kids' friends into their families, especially those who do not have the influence of Godly adults in their lives. We understand how the concept of adoption works culturally. Even as I write this book, one of the most popular television shows on cable television is *Long Lost Family*,[186] a program that "follows the stories of people who have, for one reason or another, experienced long term separation from members of their family and are seeking to be reunited with them." Peggy and I often opened our home to our kids' friends, which allowed us to build growing relationships with them as individuals. It's been decades since our children were teenagers, but some of our close relationships with their friends remain to this day. It will be important for churches to be proactive about this, instead of either waiting for it to happen or not to happen. I am afraid that many new believers have fallen away from the church because the existing church members failed to include them in the family.

I highly encourage church leaders to prayerfully think this through. How can you successfully and effectively assimilate the so called "spiritual orphans" into your church family?

Advice for Church Leaders when Working with Kids from Dysfunctional, Non-Traditional, or Weak Families:

I will conclude this Conversation with some practical advice for church leaders to consider when working with young people from households that are not spiritually strong.

1. <u>Present/preach the Gospel</u>. I said this before, but our ministry strategy must begin and end with the Gospel.

People are desperate for "Good News" and we have the life-changing resource of Scripture to share with them. Pastors should make the clear and creative exposition of the Bible a top priority. It will be from the Text that provides the opportunity to talk about life's most important issues. People do not need more stories, drama, technology, or entertainment. They need the Gospel. If the church can utilize those methods to communicate the truth of God's Word, that's fine; but if those things are the main focus, how is the church any different from what culture can offer? The difference must be our Message.

2. Plan purposeful, quality evangelistic events and programs. I have found that people from today's lost world will still respond positively to creative and culturally-relevant events and functions. It will be important to do some research in each community and area to determine what kind of events would "work" there. The real advantage of effective evangelistic events is that the activity provides something to which God's people can to invite their friends, neighbors, relatives, coworkers, and others. Plus, these events can demonstrate to the people that the church is there and that it is concerned about the needs of the community.

3. Train and encourage Godly kids to reach their friends. Here's another tactic I am convinced still works, and that is the importance of training young people who are already a part of the church to reach out to their friends. Maybe it has always been true that kids can reach other kids. Pastors and youth workers (and Christian parents for that matter) would do well to teach their kids a specific method of sharing the Gospel. It gives them confidence to have a plan or an approach that they can use in their personal conversations with unsaved people. Don't let them think that a specific outline or "plan of salvation" is what they have to use. The important thing

is to help them have the confidence and the tools they need to share the Gospel with others.

4. Hold equipping ministries. It's time to make God's Word practical—and frankly, we just need to do what It says.[187] Ephesians 4:12 says that pastor-teachers are given to the church, *"for the equipping of the saints for the work of ministry, for the edifying of the body of Christ."* I'll say it again, ministries that *equip,* train, or prepare God's people to serve Him are in rare supply in so many churches today. We must reverse this trend and begin to train people to serve Him. This familiar passage (and I admit I have referred to it several times already in this book) indicates that individual spiritual maturity and church growth are the results of the *"equipping of the saints."* This step is so important in today's needy culture. The importance of preparation and training in specific areas of life and ministry is undeniably essential.

5. Provide and publicize a safe, caring environment. Creating a safe place for kids has never been more important than it is today. Every day the news reports are filled with stories of abuse and exploitation of young people. The lack of trust is perhaps at an all-time high due to the devastating and destructive influences of sinful adults who have preyed on minors. We must shatter that stereotype by doing everything possible to create safe environments where real ministry can genuinely happen. Protecting our ministries is vital so that God can use us to demonstrate His love to today's hurting people. Church leaders must research and then implement the requirements of local and state child protection laws into the very core of today's ministries. Don't forget that background checks and legal clearances for all church workers who are involved in the lives of children and teens are a must. Plus, the use of modern technology, such as video cameras, to create a public

accessibility to what happens in church ministries may also prove to be necessary.

6. <u>Offer training and counseling for parents and families</u>. As I indicated above, training courses for parents and other family members can provide an excellent opportunity for churches today to reach out to their communities. Make sure these sessions are led by qualified and experienced facilitators who have the ability to creatively teach practical life skills from a strong Biblical perspective. Also, a church-based counseling ministry may be another open door for an expanded ministry into the lives of weak and dysfunctional households. Again, make sure your church does its homework to ensure that the potential counseling ministry is both Biblical and legal in nature. Church leaders should also explore what insurance coverage is needed before embarking on these initiatives that reach out to dysfunctional or weak households.

7. <u>Use church facilities and property for the community</u>. In my travels around the country, I found so many church buildings that sit idle for most of the week. In fact, as churches cease having programs like Sunday School, evening services, mid-week prayer meetings—and utilize small group ministries in homes instead—many of the church facilities are being used less and less. One blogger from *Christianity Today* recently stated, "If you own a building—especially if you're one of the growing number of churches that own a too-big building for your shrinking congregation—be relentless about finding creative ways to utilize the space as often as possible. For many of our churches it's 'Use It Or Lose It' time. As in, use the building or lose the church; facility, people... everything." [188] I've often wondered why churches don't give opportunities for the community to use their buildings, or at least offer programming for community outreach endeavors in the church building instead of

letting it remain unused. I think it's time to rethink the stewardship[189] of church facilities—especially as that usage provides an opportunity to reach out into the surrounding community.

8. <u>Develop strong inter-generational children's and youth ministries</u>. The rapidly increasing number of kids from non-traditional, weak, or dysfunctional households is a mandate to the church to be quite purposeful about developing inter-generational connections. So many of today's children and young people will crave healthy and growing personal relationships with caring and Godly adults. All peer ministries of the church (children's ministry, youth ministry, young adult ministry, senior citizens ministry, etc.) must work diligently to integrate a team of significant adults to carefully and slowly build interpersonal connections within the structure of those ministries AND throughout all other programming efforts of the church. In other words, it is vitally important for the children's and youth ministries to include a strategy for developing inter-generational relationships. Plus the main worships services, the all-church fellowship events, outreach, and missionary endeavors should be inter-generational in design and in practice in order to effectively reach out to today's post-Christian and post-church culture.

9. <u>Church leaders must get visibly involved in their communities</u>. It's time for pastors and other church leaders to get out of the office and into the community. It will be increasingly important for leadership team members to model, then motivate and teach the church to reach out to the growing number of dysfunctional and weak households in the area surrounding the church. This will be important in urban, suburban, and even rural areas, because as I already stated in this book, the trend away from the traditional nuclear family is booming in today's society. Involvement in the

community could range from habitual visits in a local coffee shop or family restaurant, to volunteering in a local school, to running for public office, to serving as a police or fire department chaplain, or in helping to organize community events. The important thing is to get out of the church building and make intentional relationships with unsaved and unchurched members of the community. This will help identify the real issues in your community and will provide contacts and opportunities to share the Gospel.

A few years ago, my wife and I, along with our son and daughter-in-law and a few other team members made a short-term missions trip to Durban, South Africa. During our time there, one of our host missionaries took us into one of the "slum" settlements (or "shanty towns") that are all too common in that country, even following the anti-apartheid movement that took place in the early 1990s.[190] Our quick visit certainly does not qualify me as any kind of expert on that nation's culture. But I would like to relay something we witnessed there. There is a phenomenon in those villages that is called a "child-headed family,"[191] where minor children or adolescents become the head of their households due to the absence or death of both parents (largely because of the AIDS epidemic there). Seeing these children take on the adult responsibilities of their younger siblings broke our hearts and gave us a vivid real-life illustration of the importance of God's church living out His command to *"love your neighbor as yourself."*[192]

Our culture today may not be experiencing the "child-headed family" that we observed firsthand in South Africa, but the rise of kids without any, or with very little, spiritual direction from adults at home is here—and, as Christ tarries, this situation is going to grow.

Our world is facing an unprecedented avalanche of "spiritual orphans"—members of the next generation who may or may not have some type of physically-present family structure in place, but who do not have a spiritual support system in their lives. The next generation needs a family of caring, Godly adults to invest in their lives. This is true for kids in poor family situations, and it is also true for young people from strong Christian families as well. The church must be a family where Godly adults demonstrate Christ's sacrificial love to the next generation, and where Christian kids find other Christian kids who have the courage to stand up together for Christ.

So, let's finish our conversation by talking about how to make this work in your church.

"...So that the servant of God may be thoroughly equipped for every good work."
2 Timothy 3:17 (NIV)

Conversation #10

Action Steps: How to Make This Work In Your Family and In Your church.

I mentioned this thought earlier in the book, but it's important to revisit this concept before we conclude our conversation about encouraging the next generation toward spiritual maturity. Raising kids is not a formula. It's definitely not like buying a cake mix, where we dutifully mix the proper ingredients and bake it for the exact amount of time, and unsurprisingly, out comes a cake. There's nothing predictable about raising children to be spiritually-mature adults. (In God's sovereignty, He may allow young people, even from the most consistent Christian homes and the most God-honoring churches, to rebel and to take a personal, sinful path away from God instead. Although that is definitely not what we want for our kids!)

Yet, God never intended His church or Christian parents to be nonchalant about the process of working with young people. Within the very nature of both institutions is the responsibility of reproducing our faith in the lives of the next generation. Parenting is hard work—and so is ministry![193] As I have emphasized over and over again in this book, both the church and Christian parents have the God-given responsibility to help kids grow toward spiritual maturity.

Raising kids is not necessarily predictable, but it should be intentional. Christian parents must set Biblical priorities for their families, and likewise, church leaders must faithfully communicate God's Word and effectively equip God's people so the next generation grows up to go on for God. We don't want them to walk away from God as young adults. Both institutions must do everything possible to encourage them toward long-term spiritual maturity.

So, how does this work? Practically speaking then, what do we do now?

I want to share 13 spiritual practices that both churches and parents can develop and encourage in the lives of young people to help them grow in their walks with God. But before we dig in to that answer, let's get back to the basics so that I can set the groundwork for that discussion. Square one, if you will, is to remember this is God's work. The church and the family are His ideas. These are not man-made inventions in some feeble attempt to do something we do not have the ability to do. Spiritual maturity does not mean living independently from God—just the opposite. It means realizing that as His people, we must rely totally upon Him and His grace. So if spiritual growth and maturity is what we want for our kids, we must understand that this entire process begins and continues by relying completely upon Him![194]

We also must remember that the Bible has already given us the educational process by which we are to communicate our commitment to emerging generations. We have already talked about this briefly as well, but Deuteronomy 6:6-9 is an important strategy:

> *And these words which I command you today shall be in your heart. You shall teach them diligently to your children, and shall talk of them when you sit in your house, when you walk by the way, when you lie down, and when you rise up. You shall bind them as a sign on your hand, and they shall be as frontlets between your eyes. You shall write them on the doorposts of your house and on your gates.*

Every indication from the text is that this set of instructions was given to the entire faith community in Israel—

parents obviously, but also to the nation as a whole.[195] In other words, teaching the next generation is to be a part of everything we do. It is something we do all the time. It's that important. It must not be something we segregate into a compartmentalized, silo-like structure. Neither is this something that only a specific number of interested or qualified people should do. It's something that permeates life. Parents AND church leaders need to grasp and hang onto this strategic, instructive principle. Parents understand that raising kids does not happen just one day per week. Likewise, leaders in our faith communities today (individual local churches) must also understand that the discipleship of young people does not just happen one day per week either. We're talking about life here—24/7. That's how it is supposed to work.

Building Our Practices Around Biblical Priorities: The Importance of Spiritual Disciplines

The next step is for Christian parents and church leaders to identify the priority items to put in their "grocery carts." (Remember our discussion around that illustration in Conversation #7?)

It has very important for Christian parents and church leaders to work together to build Godly habits or spiritual disciplines in the lives of kids when they are young. It has been my experience that when church leaders and Christian parents together reinforce the idea of teaching spiritual disciplines, then young people are more likely to grow into adulthood with those behaviors still a part of their lives. Our kids desperately need God-honoring and Biblically-based habits in their lives that will continue to guide them throughout childhood, through their teenage years, and then into their adult lives.

Again, the Bible provides this instruction in 1 Timothy 4:7 when it says to *"exercise yourself toward godliness."* The English word *"exercise"* used by the Apostle Paul in that verse is a translation of our English word for "gymnasium,"[196] a term that implies training, discipline, and a routine. An essential responsibility of Christian parents is to teach children basic spiritual disciplines when they are young, so that they grow up practicing those things as habits all the way through adulthood.

I noticed a rather hypocritical practice in some of the churches I visited that deserves some attention as we discuss the idea of building on-going spiritual disciplines into the lives of kids. Why do we encourage children to memorize Scripture verses and passages, and why do we train teenagers to have daily devotions or "Quiet Time" (personal time each day in God's Word), when we never talk to adults about those same spiritual disciplines? That seems rather duplicitous to me. We shouldn't forget that today's emerging generations grew up in the era of "reality television," which everyone knows are contrived situations designed to look authentic for the TV audience. Today's young people will ask, "If spiritual disciplines are important for me, why aren't the current adults practicing them?" Authenticity should transcend generations.   This is exactly why we want to build God-honoring habits into the lives of young people (and adults, by the way), so that they will grow up continuing to practice those habits.

There is a useful, real-life illustration of how this works from the life of Timothy in 2 Timothy 3:15. Paul reminds Timothy, *"from childhood you have known the Holy Scriptures, which are able to make you wise for salvation through faith which is in Christ Jesus."* One of the things that Timothy's parents did right was to teach him the Word of God. The word *"childhood"* in this passage actually means newborn, infant, or baby.[197] It's obvious from the Biblical story of Timothy that this early childhood habit of learning the Scriptures lasted throughout his entire life.

There is another important spiritual discipline that was developed at an early age in Timothy's life, and that was the importance of church. Acts 16:1-5 tells us he grew up as a church kid with a good testimony in front of the other believers in the Christian community. But, the end of Timothy's story in the Bible can be found in 2 Timothy, which again is the last letter chronologically we have from the pen of the Apostle Paul.[198] Paul probably wrote this book from a dungeon prison in Rome. It's interesting to note that Paul did not write this particular epistle to a church or a group of churches. Instead he sent it to a student—a young man who was just starting in ministry. At this point in church history, Timothy was serving as a pastor in the city of Ephesus. This one-time church kid grew up to become a pastor—an elder in a strategic cross-cultural city, leading a key local church. The regimen of Timothy's early life—involvement in church—had become a lifetime practice.

To assist readers in the practicality of what I am saying here, I took the opportunity during my travels to pinpoint some of the key practices that Godly parents AND effective churches seemed to do mutually. In other words, I looked for specific action steps that both parties were implementing with kids. My goal was to develop a list of the daily routines that parents, church leaders, and even individual young people could duplicate in life if they were serious about what we are talking about in this book.

Please understand I am not saying that implementing a list of habits equals Godliness. As author Jerry Bridges in *The Practice of Godliness* puts it, Godliness "is not an activity; it is an attitude toward God."[199] So while we know that implementing habits from a simple list does not necessarily give us a right attitude towards God, it is surely helpful to develop practices that focus our hearts and our attitudes on God.

In that vein, let me share a list of 13 practices I have observed that should be essential in the lives of young people to help them grow up and go on for God. After countless conversations with church leaders and visits to churches, and after talking with multiple parents, teenagers and young adults, this is the list of mutual spiritual disciplines I compiled:
* Daily time with God
* Bible memory
* The importance of preaching and teaching the Bible
* Learning Biblical theology
* Outreach/evangelism
* Active participation in church
* Ministry/service / Giving
* Prayer
* Fellowship and the importance of Godly friends
* Godly adult mentors

- Discipleship
- Developing Biblical convictions

The chart on the following page shows the list of these 13 practices. Plus, I have included simple and practical action steps for both Christian parents and church leaders. I encourage readers to work down through the chart, almost as a list of *best practices*, to see the helpful suggestions from several other fellow-strugglers in this process of raising children.

Going On For God

Life is comprised of a series of key milestones. Quite a few of these markers today are cultural or sociological in nature, and many of them seem associated with being or becoming an adult. They range from high school and college graduation, finding a full-time job, securing a place to live, to getting married, or having children. A new word comprising many of these cultural indicators has recently become popular with contemporary urban linguists. The term is "adulting"[200]—to engage in the duties and responsibilities of fully-developed individuals; or simply, to do things that are expected of adults. This term has become somewhat popular especially describing the behavior of Millennials over just the past few years.

I know there is much more to the process of growing to spiritual maturity than what I could possibly explain and describe here, but perhaps it works to adopt the concept of "adulting" and apply it to this conversation. There may actually be something to the notion of "spiritual adulting"—another fairly new idea with over 350,000 hits on a recent Google search.[201] Maybe this new term fits precisely with what the Apostle Paul had in mind when he wrote to the believers in Ephesus about *growing up.*[202]

God never intended spiritual maturity to be an elective. There comes a time when God's people need to grow up. I understand Bergler's idea of "The Juvenilization of American Christianity" that he so adequately presented in his recent books.[203] He observes an all-too-real trend in the church today:

GOING ON FOR GOD: ENCOURAGING THE NEXT GENERATION...

Actions Steps For Parents	PRIORITY ITEMS	Action Steps For Churches
Build a Habit of Personal Devotions	Daily Time With God	Provide Resource for Church-Wide Personal Devotions
Encourage Children to Memorize Key Passages of Scripture	Bible Memory	Motivate for Church-Wide Scripture Memory
Be Consistent in Participation in Preaching & Teaching Ministries	Preaching / Teaching	Expository Preaching & Biblical Literacy Curriculum
Find Ways to Help Children Learn Truth & Encourage Them to Participate in Church Teaching Ministries	Theology	Set Preaching Plan & Educational Ministries to Teach Systematic Bible Doctrine
Model the importance of Sharing One's Faith & Provide Evangelistic Opportunities	Outreach / Evangelism	Teach All Ages How to Share Their Faith & Provide Opportunities for Evangelistic Outreach
Be Consistent About Church Attendance & Help Children Build "Sweat-Equity"	Church Participation	Communicate Clear Reason for Why All Church Functions Are Held
Model Serving & Look for Whole-Family Means of Service	Ministry / Service	Provide Opportunities for God's People to Serve and Use Gifts & Abilities
Model Generosity & Be Consistent About Giving to God's Work	Giving	Teach on Biblical Stewardship & Communicate About Use of Church Funds
Develop a Prayer List of Important Family & "Body of Christ" Matters to Take to God	Prayer	Teach on the Subject of Prayer & Provide Opportunities for Church-Wide Prayer Meetings
Help Kids Find Good Christian Friends & Teach the Importance of Inter-Generational Connections	Fellowship / Friends	Balance Peer Ministries with Intentional Inter-Generational Connections
Help Teenagers Identify and Build Relationships with Godly Older Adults	Godly Adult Mentors	Teach on the Importance of Mentoring and Provide Opportunities for Mentoring in Ministry
Encourage Young People in Discipleship Relationships	Discipleship	Organize and Implement an Intentional Discipling Process
Teach Children Biblical Convictions & to Stand for Truth	Convictions / Bible Reasons	Help Reinforce Parents' Biblical Convictions

Too many people who claim to be followers of Christ are staying put in a juvenile world, which means they are quite likely to walk away from a lifetime of commitment to Him. To explain his concept a little bit more, I will borrow the title of an interview with Bergler in *Christianity Today:* "It's time for the church to grow up."[204]

Spiritual maturity is much more than an idea or an unachievable notion. It is real, and it is exactly what God wants from His people. Moving people toward Godliness is not arbitrary, nor is it subjective. This is what the Apostle Paul wrote about in 1 Timothy 2:2; 3:16; 4:7; 4:8; 6:6; 6:11; and in Titus 1:1; 2:11-13—and it's what the Apostle Peter proclaimed in 2 Peter 1:3 and 3:10-12. We (Christian parents and the church together) must be about the business of encouraging our young people toward what Christ wants them to be.

We also must remember that spiritual growth, much like physical growth, is intended by God to be a process. Statistically, most people come to Christ when they are young,[205] and then grow in Christ as they progress through life. Humanly speaking, there are probable times of stagnation and plateau. Perhaps there are even times when true believers either drift away from God or fall into sin, so that genuine spiritual growth does not happen. But, God wants growth to be a progression or a journey[206]—relying on His Holy Spirit, working through those human issues before the Lord in His Word, confessing sin to Him, and seeking to become more and more like His Son.[207] His goal for all of us is continued spiritual growth. Parents and church leaders alike must never forget then that what we're looking for is the end result.

It's also important to remember that progress toward spiritual maturity, again like physical growth, requires nutrients. Nothing grows without being fed. That's true with farmer's crops and household plants. It's also true with babies and children. That's why 1 Peter 2:2 says, "As *newborn babes, desire the pure milk of the word, that you may grow thereby.*" Paul puts it this way in 2 Timothy 3:16-18: "*All Scripture is given by inspiration of God, and is profitable for doctrine, for reproof, for correction, for instruction in righteousness, that the man of God may be complete, thoroughly equipped for every good work."*

So we need to go back to the pressing question I asked at the beginning of Conversation #1, "What do we want for our kids?" For me it's personal. I've mentioned my family several times in this book. Our own children are now all adults and are actively living for the Lord. Now as I write this book, my wife and I have eight grandchildren. We pray every day that they'll ALL grow up and go on for God over the long haul. It's not good enough for us that they stay active in children's Sunday School or youth group until they graduate from high school, and then go off on their own, away from God and away from the church, until sometime in the distant future when perhaps they may decide on their own to come back to Him.

Plus, I have invested over four decades of my life actively involved in youth ministry. Over those years, I have literally met thousands and thousands of kids. They've been in our churches and my youth groups, or in camps, retreats, or youth events where I have been the speaker. They've been in the youth conferences I have organized, or they've used the curriculum that I wrote. And I care about the lives of these young people.

But now as I conclude this conversation with you, I pray I have faithfully communicated the Gospel to them and that I've consistently modeled Christ in front of them. I pray they've had other adults in their lives who have mentored and discipled them, and I pray the churches they have attended have pointed them to Christ. Also, I pray I have encouraged them toward spiritual maturity and that they'll grow up and go on God!

Please join me in making this a top priority in our homes and churches!

Conclusion

As I close, let me tell you about another kid. You may know him too.

Like the other young man I wrote about in the beginning of this book, he grew up as a church kid as well. His mom and grandmother were believers, and they made sure he participated in church and church activities. They also made sure he memorized Scripture and spent time in God's Word every day so that he would understand how Biblical truth applied to day-to-day situations. Some of his close family members were Christ followers, but every indication was that his dad was not. In fact, his parents had a mixed marriage. They were from different cultural backgrounds, and probably different religious perspectives as well. In many ways, this young man was from somewhat of a dysfunctional home.

This kid had a great reputation in front of other believers and was highly recommended by older Christians for inclusion in a variety of ministry positions. He came to Christ through the ministry of a key Christian leader and was selected by that leader to accompany him on a traveling ministry team.

He grew up to be greatly used by God in a variety of different places even through quite difficult times and dangerous situations. Although probably somewhat of an introvert, this kid ultimately became a pastor in a large metropolitan, cross-cultural city and continued to serve the Lord faithfully even though he was probably timid and fearful.

According to reports, this young man, who grew up in a dysfunctional family and who was apparently quite sickly, eventually lost his life as a martyr—as someone who was willing to make the ultimate sacrifice to stand up for Christ. He grew up to go on for God—no matter what.

Of course, you know that this story is from the Bible as well. This kid's name was Timothy[208] and the narrative about his life and testimony begins when we are introduced to him in Acts

16. His story is interwoven throughout quite a few New Testament books. The Biblical timeline of his life concludes for us in the Apostle Paul's Epistle, 2 Timothy—which, as I already mentioned, is the last book we have from Paul.

The story of Timothy, like John Mark whom we talked about in the introduction to this book, is significant because he too was a church kid, went through some difficult life experiences, and ultimately grew up as someone who went on for God as an adult. Yes, he had to overcome some level of confusion and chaos in his family life and he certainly had to face some difficult cultural barriers. But he didn't walk away from God, and he didn't walk away from church. In fact, Timothy's story is one of commitment and loyalty to God and God's work in the world.

Every indication from Scripture is that Timothy grew up and lived faithfully for the Lord over the long haul. Paul wrote in 1 Corinthians 4:17 that he was "faithful" and someone with "proven character" in Philippians 2:22.

But, perhaps the most telling Scriptural reference about this young man's character is what the text tells us in 2 Timothy 1:5 where Paul says he calls *"to remembrance the genuine faith that is in you, which dwelt first in your grandmother Lois and your mother Eunice, and I persuaded is in your also."* Of course, this is a passage that is often used during Mother's Day messages about the faithful example of Timothy's Mom and Grandmother, and certainly their testimony is to be applauded because of their authenticity. But please note that the emphasis in this verse is not upon his family members. Twice in this one verse, Timothy himself, is commended for *his* "genuine faith."

The focus of this verse is *Timothy's* genuine (real, sincere, without hypocrisy, unfeigned, un-faked) faith. It is probably no coincidence here that Timothy grew up to go on for God. Unquestionably, he was influenced by the example of these Godly women in his life—even though he was from a culturally mixed, and probably spiritually-confusing home situation.

The Bible is clear that this young man was mentored by the Apostle Paul as well. Timothy "carefully followed" (see 2 Timothy 3:10-17) the example of this man of God through a wide variety of difficult life experiences. And there's no doubt that he was greatly impacted by the Word of God throughout his life (see 2 Timothy 3:15), and that he learned how to apply Biblical principles in practical life situations (see 2 Timothy 3:16-17). It is obvious that he grew up with God-honoring influences, so that he would end up as an "example"[209] for others to follow.

Let's remember that Timothy grew up to go on for God. His faith was personal. It wasn't just his Mom's or Grandmother's faith—it was real; it was his own.

And, isn't that what we want for our kids today as well?

"...to Him be glory in the church by Jesus Christ to all generations, forever and ever. Amen." Ephesians 3:21

APPENDIX 1:
Practical Ideas to Help Kids Grow Up and Go On For God

Practical Ideas for Pastors, Youth Workers, and Other Church Leaders:

- Invite older adults to share their story (testimony) with the youth group or young adult group in your church.
- Schedule a time for mature teenagers to participate in all of the ministries of the church (e.g., attend deacons' meetings, etc.) and report back to the other teenagers.
- Produce "baseball card" sized prayer cards for each teen and young adult (include a digital photo and brief bio information) in the church and give to the senior citizens class for prayer. (At least give the older adults a list and some pertinent information about each young person for prayer.)
- Schedule and plan inter-generational table game nights with simple refreshments.
- Recruit older adults to be mentors to begin inter-generational conversations and relationships in church foyer.
- Offer inter-generational "Titus 2" classes or meetings on specific issues relating to marriage, children, and other practical topics. Give older adults opportunities to mentor younger adults.
- Plan and schedule equipping ministries for parents in your church.
- Involve teens and young adults alongside adults in all public ministries—for example, greeters, parking lot attendants, ushers, worship team, tech team, etc.

- Talk with your church attorney about lowering the voting age in your church constitution—and then follow through with this decision.
- Be intentional about hosting inter-generational activities and events, where the various generations have the opportunity to actually connect.
- Take senior adults on a "field trip" to visit the youth group meetings and worship times.
- Think about ways to include older adults as youth workers or children's workers.
- Schedule and motivate people for inter-generational prayer meetings and small group Bible studies.
- Plan and take inter-generational missions trips.
- Be committed to getting involved in outreach in your community.
- Contact Mel about scheduling a "Going On For God" seminar in your church for church leaders and Christian parents. (See www.GoingOnForGod.com.)

Practical Ideas for Senior Citizens Gatherings to Become Inter-Generational:

- Encourage older adults to greet young people in the church foyer.
- Give significant older adults opportunities to share their story (testimony) in youth group or young adult meetings.
- Invite select senior adults to be involved in teaching young people from time to time.
- Motivate older students to pray specifically (by name) for young people in your church—and then schedule opportunities for them to meet those young people.
- Recruit some older adults to serve as youth workers or children's workers in your church.
- Encourage older adults to communicate specific encouragements to young people.
- Plan and schedule inter-generational table game nights or other fellowship times.

- Be intentional about providing ways for the generations to connect and build relationships.
- Schedule and motivate people for inter-generational prayer meetings.

Practical Ideas to Help Kids Gain Loyalty/Sweat Equity in the Local Church

- Today's young people are very social and justice conscious—provide opportunities for them to be actively involved in the ways your church meets the needs of your community.
- Teach young people to give and tithe to the church.
- Investigate ways to lower the voting age in your church constitution so that teenagers can participate in church business.
- Be intentional about teaching young people about your church's business meetings and leadership structure.
- Schedule and plan inter-generational work projects at the church.
- Make sure that all ministries of the church include inter-generational serving and mentoring.
- Provide ways for young people to be involved in all public ministries of the church (greeters, parking lot attendants, ushers, worship team, tech team, etc.)
- Help young people build relationships with other senior leaders in your church (in addition to the youth ministry staff).
- Motivate kids to pray specifically for your church and church leaders.
- Be intentional about involving young people in your church's missionary endeavors.
- Share with the young people that the church leaders are encouraging older adults to greet them and get to know them in the church foyer.
- Involve emerging generations in the big picture of what your church is doing in your community, your area, and around the world.

Practical Ideas for Christian Parents to Help Kids Grow Up to Go On for God

- Commit your family to the ministries of your church that feature: God's Word, worship, service, fellowship, giving, and evangelism. (Don't feel guilty for not being involved in *everything*.)
- Don't allow your kids to become "over involved" in extra-curricular activities at the expense of their involvement in church and youth group.
- Identify key spiritual disciplines that you will build as habits in the lives and schedules of your kids (daily time with God, prayer, Bible memory, preaching and teaching of God's Word, participating in church, ministry and service, giving, fellowship, etc.)
- Be intentional about building five other influential, Godly adults into the lives of your kids.
- Allow your children to invite other Christian kids into your home.
- Involve your kids in God's mission—outreach into your community and global missions.
- Find ways to involve your kids in missions trips.
- Do "all family" serving projects—do service or ministry projects together as a family.
- Teach your kids to rely on God's resources. Raise your children in humility.
- Get parenting help if needed.
- Do all you can to reach out to "spiritual orphans" and other kids from dysfunctional families in your church and community.

APPENDIX 2:
Practical Mentoring Ideas

Introduction: The following list contains simple ideas for developing inter-generational mentoring connections, keeping in mind that people have varying amounts of extra time in their schedules. Remember that the real beauty of mentoring is that it doesn't require a huge amount of time on the part of the mentor. Growing and healthy relationships can develop even if you don't have much time to invest. Remember that real mentoring is "doing what you do, just doing it with someone younger." This list is designed to be a springboard to your own creativity. The key is to reach out to young people in an effort to build connections between the generations.

If the adults say, "I have no extra time to invest."
- Add specific young people to your personal prayer list and pray faithfully for them.
- Begin a non-threatening conversation with young people in the church foyer.
- Greet teenagers and young adults with a big smile at church or when you see them elsewhere.
- Ask them for a prayer request and then pray for them right then.
- Share a blessing or prayer request with them.
- Sit near young people in church services.
- Offer to take them with you on an errand (like shopping, picking up supplies, etc.).
- Ask key young people to help you with a project.
- Invite them to your home for a meal with your family.
- Meet them at a restaurant. (You have to eat, anyway.)
- Give them something meaningful to you (like a card, a book or CD).

- Sponsor them financially for a youth group activity, missions trip, etc.

If the adults say, "I have about 15 extra minutes a week."
- Write them a note of encouragement.
- Send an e-mail or text message.
- Give them a quick phone call.
- Offer to drive them home from youth group, church, or an activity. (Make sure to follow your church's "child protection policy.")
- Initiate one-on-one conversations before or after services. (You can start by asking them about their week.)
- Brag on the young person to their parents.
- Pray for a specific need every day – and let them know you are praying.
- Compliment them in front of someone else.
- Congratulate them on a recent accomplishment.

If the adults say, "I have 30 extra minutes a week."
- Discuss your devotions together.
- Go to 30 minutes of their event (sports, drama, concert, etc.).
- Offer to drop in to see them in youth group.
- Meet them in a non-threatening location for accountability or prayer.
- Drop in on them at work (if appropriate).
- Pray for their specific needs each day.
- Provide transportation to and from an activity or work. (Make sure to follow your church's "child protection policy.")
- Memorize a passage of Scripture together.

If the adults say, "I have 2 extra hours a week."
- Find something you have in common and do that together.
- Visit in the students' homes. (Again, make sure to follow your church's "child protection policy.")

- Invite them to an evening in your home. (Play table games or other simple activities together.)
- Take them out to eat.
- Take their parents out to dinner.
- Help them with homework.
- Do a service project, ministry, hobby, or craft together (golf, cooking, working on cars, etc.).
- Pop a bag of popcorn and hang out.
- Go shopping together.
- Wash and wax their car.
- Listen to music or Podcasts together.
- Discuss a spiritual or theological question and search the Scriptures for the answer.
- Go on a simple activity together (shopping, miniature golfing, bowling, etc.).
- Have a Bible study together.
- Take a gift to a needy friend together.

If the adults say, "I have 4 extra hours a week."
- Play a round of golf or work on a craft or hobby together.
- Go on a walk or a hike.
- Go to a ball game or musical concert (let them select the artist).
- Make a video.
- Volunteer at a mission.
- Read/discuss a Bible study book.
- Teach the young person a new skill: how to change a tire, how to knit, etc.
- Give emerging adults the opportunity to teach you something new.
- Participate in a church work day together.

If the adults say, "I have 10 extra hours a week."
- Go on a camp-out – or other overnight retreat together. (Once again, make sure to follow your church's "child protection policy.")
- Clean/organize something together.
- Paint or build something together.

- Wash and clean the pastor's car.
- Organize a food drive and deliver to a needy family.
- Start a new ministry at church together.

If the adults say, "I have 20 extra hours a week."

- "Get a life!"

Note: Some of these ideas are suggested in *The Mentoring Handbook* published by Youth Alive Student Ministries, Bethesda Baptist Church in Brownsburg, Indiana and Lake Ann Baptist Camp, Lake Ann, Michigan. Some of these ideas can also be found in Doug Field's book *Purpose-Driven Youth Ministry* published by Zondervan.

APPENDIX 3:
I want busy kids In Our student ministry

Youth workers need to stop whining!

Students are busy, active, and stressed. The result of this activity is that they do not have enough time to attend our meetings and church. Many youth workers are discouraged—and often feel rejected. Soon many express discouragement by complaining about the kids' lack of commitment to God or interest in the church.

I have heard youth workers who make busyness of students a spiritual issue. Activity becomes sinful because we have tossed the gauntlet of proof to the kids. If they are committed to Christ, they must prove it by attending church more and attending other activities less. If students do not respond as prescribed, they must not be committed to the Lord.

Today many churches and student ministries have given up on the idea and action of reaching busy students. Reaching these kids is not even on their radar. Not long ago, on a weeknight, I attended a wrestling match at our local high school. Going on at the same time - a swim meet, winter color guard, and a basketball game. Busy kids and their parents were scattered throughout the athletic wing of the high school. To my knowledge, I was the only local church representative in the school that evening. I believe we should change our attitudes and actions toward busy kids and begin to devise ways to reach and minister to them.

We need to stop whining!

Students are busy—and if our culture remains unchanged, there will be no turning back to the good old days when kids spent time at home and our church youth group was the "only show in town." Kids spend more time away from home than ever before. Our high school students can be found training for sports at 5:45 in the morning. "Zero hour" class begins at 7 AM. School ends at 3:15 when bands, choirs, sports, and jobs all demand the time and attention of students. Our Fellowship of Christian Athletes *Huddle* even meets one day every week at 7 AM. During the week, high-involvement students from our school may never see the sun from October through February! Kids *are* busy.

Instead of becoming discouraged because our church or programs are not the first choice of students, we must be proactive in reaching these kids. We need to change the way we think about busy kids, and then we must change our ministry in order to reach these students more effectively. Here are some vital truths about busy kids that will help guide us as we make these personal changes.

Busy Students Are Achieving Students

I have a theory about busy kids. Generally, the kids who are the busiest are also the kids who are and will accomplish the most in school and in their lives after high school. These are the kids who are the athletes, scientists, money-makers, and movers-and-shakers in their school. They are also likely to become the movers-and-shakers in the future. Busy students are stretching for and achieving great things. These students may be the editors of the yearbook or school newspaper. They may be in the top academic 10% of their class. They are leaders in the gym, in academics, and music wing. Busy students are achieving students. I want achieving students in our church student ministry.

Busy Students Are Motivated Students

There is definitely something or someone that draws our students. They motivate them. This is almost always a good thing. A teacher, coach, or employer has given these students what someone has called a "vision of destiny." These kids have taken the challenge of becoming better than when they started. They have taken the challenge of becoming "The Best." At some point during the time we are able to come into contact with these kids, they have made the decision to do whatever it takes to be the best. They study longer and harder. They get up earlier and go to bed later. Their friends are other kids who are like them. For some reason these students are highly motivated. I want motivated kids to be a part of our student ministry.

Busy Students Are Responsible Students

The busy student has a high threshold of responsibility. They meet deadlines. They make appointments and keep them. They map out their day and they plan their week. These kids revel in the challenge of turning in a tough assignment on time and done accurately. They are precise in almost everything they do. Because of this characteristic, they easily see when the church and student ministry are sloppy, unprepared, or disorganized. Their calendar has meaning to them. It tells them when the game is, when the assignment is due, when church meets, what days they work, and how much spare time they have. They are also responsible in the sense that they take on great tasks. They are the class officers, editor, or shift manager. They are members of the campus groups who tutor children, raise money for good causes, commit to service, and plan and pull off big events. Busy students are responsible students. I want responsible students as part of our student ministry.

Busy Students Are Demanding Students

Because there is such a premium and demand for the busy students' time and energy, they often demand the same from others. That is why they usually have a circle of friends who are just as busy as them. They expect a similar commitment from their friends as they expect from themselves. These kids usually keep their commitments. They behave in a way that demonstrates their time is valuable and their relationships are valuable. The busy student responds to activities and people who understand their demanding outlook. The person who knows the way to develop and reach goals and accomplishments will influence these kids. I want demanding students as part of our student ministry.

Busy Students Are Our Students

The busy student desires to be part of something big. They also desire to be a part of our student ministry. They want to know what the church is doing even when they cannot make the meetings. They want to be part of our student ministry even though there will have to be exceptions. They will not be able to attend all of the youth meetings or church services. They still desire to be part of our ministry. These kids have similar desires as the rest of our students. They need to know that they belong, and they want to know where they belong. Busy students are our students. We should want them to be part of our student ministry.

Making Personal Changes

Understanding these truths about busy kids should lead us to the place of personal and ministry changes that we should make in order to reach these students in a more effective way. These changes may be dramatic. They may require imagination and creativity before they become an integral part of our ministries. Reaching these students will certainly require more time and energy from those of us who desire to reach them for Christ. The fact remains that we need to make some changes if we will influence this dynamic group of students.

1. **Change Our Vision**

   In order to change our vision, we need to see these students as part of a bigger picture. Until now, we have seen them as kids who fit or don't fit into *our* program. The students are busy in various activities and I want the church ministry to become one of those activities. The change takes place because I no longer demand that the activities of a student should revolve around mine, or those of the student ministry. There is no Scriptural command that I am aware of that demands that our church schedule moves into the realm of convictions.

   At every level, there are adults who have the students' ear. There are adults who motivate and inspire them to strive to accomplish great things. I want to be one of those adults. I want all student ministry workers to be those adults who inspire kids to do great things for God. Our view of worship can help to guide us. All of life is worship, 24/7; and not merely the couple of times our group meets every week. We need to teach and live that all our gifts and abilities are from the Lord. The talent that leads kids to be busy and drives them toward accomplishment is God given and the student is a steward of that talent.

Youth workers should emphasize teaching about what a Christian is and does within culture because that is where these kids spend most of their time. They have hope, joy, love, and humility because they are followers of Christ and they should demonstrate it in all they do. They **are** salt and light as they move throughout their schedule. Because of this fact, they will influence every person and every situation in which they are involved for Christ. These students will respond to big picture ideas and actions. We need to change our vision from a small picture, my church schedule, to a bigger picture that combines their schedule with ours.

2. **Change Our Direction**
   I believe that we struggle with busy students because we are sometimes moving in the wrong direction. Jesus commands us to "Go" (Matthew 28:19). He also told the disciples to be witnesses from Jerusalem to the ends of the earth (Acts 1:8). These and other Scriptures strongly imply the direction we take as we minister. That direction is out! Go, out there, over here, or beyond. When we whine that busy kids do not attend our meetings, we are saying "come"—and then we express frustration when they do not attend. Expecting kids to come is not going. Change direction and go. Going will by its nature make us busier. When working with busy kids, we must be busy just to keep up with them. This is

the point where many youth workers become resistant. We are already busy and resist the call for more.

While having coffee with a senior high youth leader, she expressed the desire that one of her students would attend and participate in meetings. I know the girl she was speaking about, so after a moment I suggested she immediately get her phone and text our friend asking to get together over coffee. If my friend was going to influence her student she had to go to her.

We need to find out how we can support our kids. We need to include them by giving information that tells them not only what they miss, but also what is in the future of your student ministry. We need to become an appointment on their calendar. Use creativity and make a point of contact with busy students.

A young man I know finished his high school academic career as the salutatorian in his class of over 500 students. As I listened to his speech at graduation, I was amazed at his clear challenge for his fellow graduates to forsake the wide path that leads to death and go with him on the "narrow way that leads to life." His mother told me that because he was busy, his youth pastor met him for breakfast every Thursday morning at 7 o'clock. The youth pastor would share the events of the church, share a key verse of Scripture, and send him to school with prayer. The youth pastor developed a specific way to be an influence on this young man. He was not demanding that his friend come and conform to the church schedule, so he changed his direction. To reach the student, he went to the student at a time when the student could meet. We need to change our direction.

3. **Change Our View of Parents**
When busy students miss youth group or church because of their activities, our first or second reaction is to

express disappointment with the student's parents. We also must raise our game in relating to parents of our student ministry. Gone are the days when mom and dad say to their child, "you will go to church because the doors are open." Parents want their student to excel in whatever they do. On the positive side, they will want their child to excel in church. They want them to meet Christ, be baptized—and attend when they are able. However, parents want the same for every activity in which their kids participate. There is not a lot of differentiation between church, youth group, school work, marching band, athletic teams, or music programs. We need to come alongside parents in all those situations and circumstances and not only our church activity.

We must become an expert at something, so we become a resource for parents and kids. God has gifted all of us with skills and abilities. Use it as a resource. We must "sell" ourselves to parents. Becoming an expert at something will help to do this. We must also sell our vision to parents. How do we view their child, their family, and what can we do through Christ and the church to walk alongside their family? We must sell our program to the parents. Why should their kids hold our church ministry as a priority? Sell it! We must seek information about the student and their family. When we do this, we can minister insightfully and effectively.

I was able to advise my youth worker friend about meeting her student for coffee because I knew her student and how she responds when adults show an interest in her. We must change our view of parents. We are not the only show in town and we must win them over by our interest, our excellence, and our love for their kids. We must win the parents.

4. Change Our Action

In order to change our action, we must be creative and courageous as we devise ways to influence busy kids. We need to honor the students' time as much as they do. Many youth workers complain about being busy when the kids they work with are at least as busy. Busy kids are organized. We need to get organized. Plan ahead. Be prepared. When we speak, we should know what we are going to say. Our student ministry should be an oasis for students. A busy student will not come to a student ministry where the leaders are poorly prepared and unmotivated.

We need to be one of the people in their lives that will motivate them to big accomplishments. This will start with Scripture and end with a program. When students give us an hour of their time, we must take better advantage of that hour! I know of a youth ministry that played gym games for the first 35 minutes of almost every meeting. A group of high achieving kids began to show up 35 minutes late. In their mind, they were on time. The program always started late, so they showed up late. Changing our action may require us to look at our meeting schedule in a different way. For a couple of years we had several kids in our group playing soccer at different schools. Since the soccer games were on our usual meeting nights, I invented the "Breakaway." When our kids played each other, the youth group met at the soccer stadium and our student ministry supported our kids. When we really change, our presence at the games may be more meaningful in the student's life than a month of meetings at the church. Change our action.

5. Change Our Expectations

Instead of expecting busy kids to be present in church every time the door is open, I expect kids to represent Jesus and our student ministry in every activity in which they are involved. I want them to attend when they are able. My expectation of the meeting changes from just something we do every week to an event to be presented as an encouragement to the student's life. We must become unpredictable in our group meetings, creatively use resources, and wisely use our time.

One girl told me that when she knows the youth group has a "throw away" meeting (games, etc.) she doesn't attend. When it is a serious meeting she makes an effort to be there. A serious meeting was a planned Bible Study, presented in a creative way that speaks to the heart of her busy life. Put more time and energy into the student ministry meeting. Pray and expect the Lord to do big things in and through these kids.

My expectation for myself changes. Strive to build points of contact with these students. Expect these kids to be world changers for God. I want to be one of the motivators in these kids' lives. They expect to do great things and I want to point them in the direction of doing those great things—for the Lord!

Additional Thoughts on Reaching Busy Kids

I think there is one other situation to look at when thinking about busy kids—their school and community. Kids are often busier when the high school and/or the church is small and located in smaller communities. I have not addressed this before, but it may even be more of an acute situation than with big churches in larger communities. By small, I mean the school would have less than 500 students. For small schools to have and perpetuate programs in music, choir, band, and athletics almost every student must participate in some extracurricular activities. These are the schools where the football lineman marches at halftime playing the trumpet in his football uniform. The cheerleader runs to the band during a basketball timeout and plays the trombone. The student's parents must chaperone and plan the "after-the-prom-party" or the school will not be able to have one. I think for the church to reach the smaller community and school they will need to adjust to these exceptional circumstances.

They will also need to adjust to have an influential ministry to their own attenders. The student ministry will need to become an actual part of the community. At times, church and school events can be the very same event. Perhaps schedule post-school events like "5th Quarters," Bible studies that begin at 10:00 PM on a Friday, movie nights that begin later in the evening. The point is to become united with community and school events.

The student ministry can come along side of parents in this situation too. Help parents plan on behalf of the church and school. Helping them with laundering the band uniforms, chaperoning dances, or cheering the kids are just a couple of ideas. The student ministry needs to imagine how they might interact with the school and families. The adults in the student ministry might go to the administration of the school and offer prayer and support. Ask how you and the church might be of help to the school during the semester or school year. You might be surprised that they will have a list of things for which they can use the help of the student ministry!

Smaller schools need a higher percentage of kids to participate to carry out effective activities. This will affect the churches in those communities. The church kids will, of necessity, be busy. Imagine the many ways your church and student ministry can come alongside the school. As we do this we will also be ministering to and assisting our church kids and their parents.

Reaching busy students is difficult, but I believe it can be done. When we begin to see and learn truths about busy kids, we are then guided to make personal changes in our lives. Change is not easy. To change something means something else must stop. Creativity and courage must be our attitude as we change vision, direction, action, and expectation.

I want busy kids in our student ministry!

NOTE: Tim Ahlgrim is a veteran youth worker, coach, speaker and writer, and is the Executive Director of Vision For Youth, Inc. Readers can reach him at: tim@visionforyouth.com. This article is used here with permission from the author.

Works Consulted

Anthony, Michael J., Michelle Anthony (Karen E. Jones, Freddy Cardoza, Michael S. Lawson, Richard R. Melick, Curt Hamner, Leon M. Blanchette, Gordon R. Coulter, James Thompson, Timothy P. Jones, Randy Stinson, Kit Rae, and David Keehn). *A Theology for Family Ministries.* Nashville, TN: B & H Academic, 2011.

Anthony, Michelle, and Marshman, Megan. *7 Family Ministry Essentials.* Colorado Springs, CO: David C. Cook, 2015.

Arnett, Jeffrey Jensen. *Emerging Adulthood: The Winding Road from the Late Teens through the Twenties.* New York: Oxford University Press, 2004.

Arzola, Fernando, Brian Cosby, Ron Hunter, Greg Stier, and Chap Clark, editor. *Youth Ministry in the 21st Century: Five Views.* Grand Rapids, MI: Baker Academic (Baker Publishing Group), 2015.

Barna, George. *Transforming Children into Spiritual Champions: Why Children Should be Your Church's #1 Priority.* Ventura, CA: Regal Books/Gospel Light, 2003.

Barna, George, and David Kinnaman. *Churchless: Understanding Today's Unchurched and How to Connect with Them: Based on Surveys by Barna Group.* Carol Stream, IL: Tyndale House, 2014.

Baucham, Voddie. *Family Driven Faith: Doing What It Takes to Raise Sons and Daughters Who Walk with God.* Wheaton, IL: Crossway, 2011.

Baucham, Voddie. *Family Shepherds: Calling and Equipping Men to Lead Their Homes.* Wheaton, IL: Crossway, 2011.

Baxter, Jeff. *Together: Adults and Teenagers Transforming the Church.* Grand Rapids, MI: Zondervan, 2010.

Bengtson, Vern L., with Norella M. Putney and Susan Harris. *Faith and Families: How Religion is Passed Down Across Generations.* Oxford: Oxford University Press, 2013.

Bergler, Thomas E. *From Here to Maturity: Overcoming the Juvenilization of American Christianity.* Grand Rapids, MI: Eerdmans, 2014.

Bergler, Thomas E. *The Juvenilization of American Christianity.* Grand Rapids, MI: William B. Eerdmans Pub., 2012.

Bisset, Tom. *Why Christian Kids Leave the Faith.* Nashville, TN: T. Nelson, 1992.

Bolsinger, Tod E. *It Takes a Church to Raise a Christian: How the Community of God Transforms Lives.* Grand Rapids, MI: Brazos (Baker Book House), 2004.

Bonhoeffer, Dietrich, and John W. Doberstein. *Life Together: The Classic Exploration of Christian Commuity.* San Francisco: HarperOne, 1954.

Brown, Scott T. *A Weed in the Church: How a Culture of Age Segregation Is Harming the Younger Generation, Fragmenting the Family, and Dividing the Church.* Wake Forest, NC: National Center for Family-Integrated Churches, 2010.

Burns, Jim, and Mike DeVries. *Partnering with Parents in Youth Ministry.* Ventura, CA: Gospel Light, 2003.

Burns, Jim, and Mike DeVries. *Partnering with Parents in Youth Ministry.* Ventura, CA: Gospel Light, 2003.

Calhoun, Mike, and Mel Walker. *The Greenhouse Project: Cultivating Students of Influence.* Schroon Lake, NY: Word of Life Fellowship, 2009.

Cannister, Mark. *Teenagers Matter: Making Student Ministry a Priority in the Church.* Grand Rapids, MI: Baker Academic, 2013.

Clark, Chap, editor. *Adoptive Youth Ministry: Integrating Emerging Generations into the Family of Faith.* Grand Rapids, MI: Baker Academic, 2016.

Clark, Chap, editor (Fernando Arzola, Brian Cosby, Ron Hunter, Greg Stier). *Youth Ministry in the 21st Century: Five Views.* Grand Rapids, MI: Baker Academic, 2015.

Clinton, Hillary Rodham. *It Takes a Village: And Other Lessons Children Teach Us.* New York: Touchstone (Simon & Schuster), 1996.

Cosby, Brian H. *Giving up Gimmicks: Reclaiming Youth Ministry from an Entertainment Culture*. Phillipsburg, NJ: P&R Pub., 2012.

Creps, Earl G. *Reverse Mentoring: How Young Leaders Can Transform the Church and Why We Should Let Them*. San Francisco, CA: Jossey-Bass, 2008.

Dalfonzo, Gina. *One By One: Welcoming the Singles in Your Church*. Grand Rapids, MI: Baker Books, 2017.

Dembowczyk, Brian. *Gospel Centered Kids Ministry: How the Gospel will Transform Your Kids, Your Church, Your community, and the World*. Nashville, TN: LifeWay Christian Resources, 2017.

Demme, Steve. *The Christian Home and Family Worship*. Litiz, PA: Building Faith Families, 2015.

Dever, Mark, and Jamie Dunlop. *The Compelling Community: Where God's Power Makes a Church Attractive*. Loveland, CO: Group, 2015.

DeVries, Mark. *Sustainable Youth Ministry: Why Most Youth Ministry Doesn't Last and What Your Church Can Do About It?* Downers Grove, IL: Inter-Varsity, 2008.

DeVries, Mark. *Family-Based Youth Ministry: Reaching the Been-There, Done-That Generation*. Downers Grove, IL: Inter-Varsity, 1994.

DeYoung, Kevin and Greg Gilbert. *What is the Mission of the Church? Making Sense of Social Justice, Shalom, and the Great Commission*. Wheaton, IL: Crossway, 2011.

DeYoung, Kevin, and Ted Kluck. *Why We Love the Church: In Praise of Institutions and Organized Religion*. Chicago: Moody, 2009.

Eckel, Mark, G. Tyler Fischer, Troy Temple, and Michael S. Wilder. *Perspectives on Your Child's Education: 4 Views*, Nashville, TN: B&H Academics, 2009.

Fields, Doug. *Purpose-Driven Youth Ministry: 9 Essential Foundations for Healthy Growth*. Grand Rapids, MI: Zondervan, 1998.

Fox, J. Mark. *Family-Integrated Church: Healthy Families, Healthy Church*. Longwood, FL: Xulon Press, 2006.

Freudenburg, Ben F., with Rick Lawrence. *The Family-friendly Church*. Loveland, CO: Vital Ministry, 1998.

Gangel, Kenneth O., and Jim Wilhoit. *The Christian Educator's Handbook on Family Life Education*. Grand Rapids, MI: Baker, 2000.

Ham, Ken (with Jeff Kinley). *Ready to Return? The Need for a Fundamental Shift in Church Culture to Save a Generation*. Green Forest, AR: Master Books, 2015.

Ham, Ken, Britt Beemer, and Todd A. Hillard. *Already Gone: Why Your Kids Will Quit Church and What You Can Do to Stop It*. Green Forest, AR: Master Books, 2009.

Harder, Mike. *Engage: A Youth Worker's Guide to Creating a Culture of Mentoring*. Kansas City, MO: Barefoot Ministries, 2012.

Haynes, Brian. *The Legacy Path: Discover Intentional Spiritual Parenting*. Nashville, TN: Randall House, 2011.

Haynes, Brian. *Shift: What It Takes to Finally Reach Families Today*. Loveland, CO: Group Pub., 2009.

Holmen, Mark, and Mark Holmen. *Church + Home: The Proven Formula for Building Lifelong Faith*. Ventura, CA: Regal, 2010.

Hunter Jr., Ron. *The DNA of D6: Building Block of Generational Discipleship*. Nashville, TN: Randall House, 2015.

Joiner, Reggie, and Carey Nieuwhof. *Parenting Beyond Your Capacity: Connect Your Family to a Wider Community*. Colorado Springs, CO: David C. Cook, 2010.

Joiner, Reggie. *Think Orange: Imagine the Impact When Church and Family Collide*. Colorado Springs, CO: David C. Cook, 2009.

Jones, Timothy P. *Family Ministry Field Guide: How Your Church Can Equip Parents to Make Disciples*. Indianapolis, IN: Wesleyan Pub. House, 2011.

Kimball, Dan. *They Like Jesus but Not the Church: Insights from Emerging Generations*. Grand Rapids, MI: Zondervan, 2007.

Kinnaman, David, and Aly Hawkins. *You Lost Me: Why Young Christians Are Leaving Church-- and Rethinking Faith*. Grand Rapids, MI: Baker, 2011.

Lyons, Gabe. *The Next Christians: The Good News about the End of Christian America.* New York: Doubleday Religion, 2010.

Lytch, Carol E. *Choosing Church: What Makes a Difference for Teens.* Louisville & London: Westminster John Knox Press, 2004.

Martineau, Mariette, Joan Weber, and Leif Kehrwald. *Intergenerational Faith Formation: All Ages Learning Together.* New London, CT: Twenty-Third Publications, 2008.

McIntosh, Gary L. *One Church Four Generations: Understanding & Reaching All Ages in Your Church.* Grand Rapids, MI: Baker, 2002.

Menconi, Peter. *The Intergenerational Church: Understanding Congregations from WWII to Www.com.* Littleton, CO: Mt. Sage, 2010.

Miller, Dan, and Jared Angaza. *Wisdom Meets Passion: When Generations Collide and Collaborate.* Nashville, TN: Thomas Nelson, 2012.

Miller, Jamie. (Dan Halvorsen, Sarah Stadler, Gretchen Miller, Scott Clements.) *Being Church.* Bloomington, MN: Consumed Publishing, 2016.

Morgan, Brock. *Youth Ministry 2017.* San Diego, CA: The Youth Cartel, 2017.

Morgan, Brock. *Youth Ministry in a Post-Christian World: A Hopeful Wake-up Call.* San Diego, CA: Youth Cartel, LLC, 2013.

Mueller, Walt. *Opie Doesn't Live Here Anymore: Where Faith, Family, and Culture Collide.* Cincinnati, OH: Standard Pub., 2007.

Nieuwhof, Carey. *Lasting Impact: 7 Powerful Conversations that Will Help Your Church Grow.* Cumming, GA: The reThink Group, 2015.

Nyquist, J. Paul., and Carson Nyquist. *The Post-Church Christian: Dealing with the Generational Baggage of Our Faith.* Chicago: Moody, 2013.

Oestreicher, Mark. *A Volunteer Youth Worker's Guide to Leading a Small Group*. Place of Publication Not Identified: Barefoot Ministries, 2013.

Oestriecher, Mark. *A Volunteer Youth Worker's Guide to Resourcing Parents*. Kansas City: Barefoot Ministries, 2013.

Olshine, David. *Youth Ministry: What's Gone Wrong and How to Get It Right*. Nashville: Abingdon, 2013.

Packard, Josh and Ashleigh Hope. *Church Refugees: Sociologists Reveal Why People Are Done with Church But Not Their Faith*. Loveland, CO: Group Books, 2015.

Powell, Kara. *The Sticky Faith Guide for Your Family: Over 100 Practical and Tested Ideas to Build Lasting Faith in Kids*. Grand Rapids, MI: Zondervan, 2014.

Powell, Kara and Chap Clark. *Sticky Faith: Everyday Ideas to Build Lasting Faith in Your Kids*. Grand Rapids, MI: Zondervan, 2011.

Powell, Kara, Brad M. Griffin, and Cheryl A. Crawford. *Sticky Faith: Practical Ideas to Nurture Long-Term Faith in Teenagers*. Grand Rapids, MI: Zondervan, 2011.

Powell, Kara, Jake Mulder, and Brad Griffin. *Growing Young: 6 Essential Strategies to Help Youth People Discover and Love Your Church*. Grand Rapids, MI: Baker Books, 2016.

Rainer, Thom S., and Eric Geiger. *Simple Church: Returning to God's Process for Making Disciples*. Nashville: B & H Publishing Group, 2011.

Rainer, Thom S., and Sam S. Rainer. *Essential Church?: Reclaiming a Generation of Dropouts*. Nashville: B & H Publishing Group, 2008.

Rainer, Thom S. *Autopsy of a Deceased Church: 12 Ways to Keep Yours Alive*. Nashville, TN: B&H Publishing Group, 2014.

Renfro, Paul, Brandon Shields, Jay Strother, and Timothy P. Jones. *Perspectives on Family Ministry: 3 Views*. Nashville, TN: B & H Academic, 2009.

Rice, Wayne. *Engaging Parents as Allies*. Cincinnati, OH: Standard Pub., 2009.

Rice, Wayne. *Reinventing Youth Ministry (Again)*. Downers Grove, IL: IVP Books, 2010.

Sasse, Ben. *The Vanishing American Adult: Our Coming-of-Age Crisis and How to Rebuild a Culture of Self-Reliance.* New York, NY: St. Martin's Press, 2017.

Shaw, Haydn. *Generational IQ: Christianity Isn't Dying, Millennials Aren't the Problem, And the Future is Bright.* Carol Stream, IL: Tyndale House, 2015.

Smith, Christian with Melinda Lundquist Denton. *Soul Searching: The Religious and Spiritual Lives of American Teenagers.* Oxford, England: Oxford University Press, 2005.

Smith, Christian with Patricia Snell. *Souls in Transition: The Religious & Spiritual Lives of Emerging Adults.* Oxford, England: Oxford University Press, 2009.

Smith, Christian with Kari Christoffersen, Hilary Davidson & Patricia Snell Herzog. *Lost in Transition: The Dark Side of Emerging Adulthood.* Oxford, England: Oxford University Press, 2011.

Stetzer, Ed, Richie Stanley, and Jason Hayes. *Lost and Found: The Younger Unchurched and the Churches That Reach Them.* Nashville, TN: B&H Pub. Group, 2009.

Stinson, Randy and Timothy Paul Jones, editors. *Trained in the Fear of God: Family Ministry in Theological, Historical, and Practical Perspective.* Grand Rapids, MI: Kregel Academic & Professional, 2011.

Stollings, Jessica. *ReGeneration: Why Connecting Generations Matters (and How to Do It).* North Charleston, SC: ReGenerations, 2015.

Strommen, Merton and Richard Hardel. *Passing on the Faith: A Radical New Model for Youth and Family Ministry.* Winona, MN: Saint Mary's Press, Christian Brothers Publications, 2000.

Taylor, Paul. *The Next America: Boomers, Millennials, and the Looming Generational Showdown.* New York: Public Affairs (Perseus), 2014.

Tripp, Paul David. *Age of Opportunity: A Biblical Guide to Parenting Teens.* Phillipsburg, NJ: P & R, 2001.

Tripp, Tedd. *Shepherding a Child's Heart.* Wapwallopen, PA: Shepherd, 1995.

Tyson, Jon. *Sacred Roots: Why the Church Still Matters*. Grand Rapids, MI: Zondervan, 2013.

Viola, Frank. *Reimagining Church: Pursuing the Dream of Organic Christianity*. Colorado Springs, CO: David C. Cook, 2008.

Walker, Mel. *Inter-Generational Youth Ministry: Why a Balanced View of Connecting the Generations Is Essential for the Church*. Chinchilla, PA: Vision For Youth Publishing/Overboard Ministries, 2013.

Walker, Mel. *Mentoring the Next Generation: A Strategy for Connecting the Generations*. Schaumburg, IL: Regular Baptist Press, 2003.

Wallace, Eric. *Uniting Church and Home: A Blueprint for Rebuilding Church Community*. Lorton, VA: Solutions for Integrating Church and Home, 1999.

Warren, Richard. *The Purpose-Driven Church: Growth without Compromising Your Message & Mission*. Grand Rapids, MI: Zondervan Pub., 1995.

Watters, Ethan. *Urban Tribes: A Generation Redefines Friendship, Family, and Commitment*. New York: Bloomsbury, 2003.

Watters, Ethan. *Urban Tribes: Are Friends the New Family?* London: Bloomsbury, 2004.

White, James Emery. *The Rise of the Nones: Understanding and Reaching the Religiously Unaffiliated*. Grand Rapids, MI: Baker, 2014.

Wilcher, Scott. *The Orphaned Generation: The Father's Heart for Connecting Youth and Young Adults to Your Church*. Chesapeake, VA: UpStream Project, 2010.

Zschech, Darlene. *The Art of Mentoring: Embracing the Great Generational Transition*. Minneapolis: Bethany House, 2011.

About the Author

Mel Walker is the president and co-founder of Vision For Youth, Inc., an international network for youth ministry. Mel is a frequent speaker (both nationally and internationally) at youth, church leadership, family life, and parenting conferences. He speaks to thousands of students, church leaders, and youth workers each year and has organized and led several regional, statewide, and national youth and youth ministry conferences and events. Mel is a graduate of Clarks Summit University (then Baptist Bible College & Seminary). He holds an Associate of Arts degree, a Bachelor of Religious Education, and Master of Ministry degree, and has done graduate work at Iowa State University and Faith Baptist Theological Seminary.

Mel and his wife, Peggy, are the parents of 3 grown children: Kristi (a missionary in Germany), Todd, and his wife, Janine, (Vision For Youth missionaries), and Travis, along with his wife, Kaci (serving as a youth pastor)—and now have 8 grandchildren. Mel and Peggy are active in Heritage Baptist Church in Clarks Summit, PA, where they co-lead the college-age young adult ministry. Mel is also the director of youth ministry at Wyoming Valley Church in Wilkes-Barre, PA.

After serving as a youth pastor in Michigan for several years, Mel then taught youth and family ministry courses and served in various administrative roles at Faith Baptist Bible College in Ankeny, Iowa, and then at Baptist Bible College and Seminary in Clarks Summit, PA. He also ministered for several years as the director of student ministries for Regular Baptist Press in Arlington Heights, Illinois—where he led in their complete revision of the youth Sunday School curriculum. He is the author of eight other books including *Inter-Generational Youth Ministry: Why a Balanced View of Connecting the Generations is*

Essential for the Church, which was also published with Overboard Ministries and Vision For Youth Publishing.

Mel is available for speaking in churches, seminars, and conferences, and consults with churches around the country on how they can effectively reach and impact emerging generations. Much more information about this book and Mel's ministry can be found at: www.GoingOnForGod.com or www.melwalker.org.

Endnotes and Biblical References Cited

1 http://www.dictionary.com/browse/inter-.

2 For further study on the life of John Mark in Scripture read: Acts 12:12, 25; 13:1-5, 13; 15:36-41; Colossians 4:10-11; Philemon 2:4; 2 Timothy 4:11; 1 Peter 5:13; and the Gospel According to Mark.

3 See Matthew 16:18.

4 See *Inter-Generational Youth Ministry: Why a Balanced View of Connecting the Generations is Essential for the Church* by Mel Walker, Overboard Ministries/Vision For Youth Publishing, 2013.

5 See the terms "emerging adulthood" and "emerging generations" used in *Emerging Adulthood: The Winding Road from the Late Teens through the Twenties* by Jeffrey Jenson Arnett, Oxford University Press, New York, 2006 (pp. 3-4).

6 *A Survey of Bible Doctrine* by Charles C. Ryrie, Moody Publishers, Chicago, 1972 (p. 140).

7 *Rediscovering Church: The Story and Vision of Willow Creek Community Church* by Lynne and Bill Hybels, Zondervan Publishing House, Grand Rapids, 1995 (p.169).

8 Bernard Weinraub. *The New York Times,* June 1998. www.nytimes.com/1998/06/18/arts/dousing-the-glow-of-tv-s-first-family-time-for-the-truth-about-ozzie-and-harriet.html.

9 Many sociologists are unsure about the exact etymology of the phrase "nuclear family." However, it is generally assumed that the term *nuclear* was used in its general meaning referring to a central entity or "nucleus" around which others collect. See en.wikipedia.org/wiki/Nuclear_family.

10 To obtain one journalist's perspective on how the family unit has been replaced in contemporary society see *Urban Tribes: A Generation Redefines Friendship, Family, and Commitment* by Ethan Watters, Bloomsbury Publishing, New York, 2003.

[11] Jonathan Merritt. *Religion News Service.* September 2013. www.jonathanmerritt.religionnews.com/2013/09/10/from-full-house-to-modern-family-ten-shows-that-forced-us-to-reimagine-the-american-family/.

[12] See en.wikipedia.org/wiki/Will_%26_Grace.

[13] For example see www.worldwideerc.org/Resources/MOBILITY articles/Pages/Day0613.aspx and www.nytimes.com/2013/11/26/health/families.html?pagewanted=all.

[14] www.wggb.com/2015/04/20/zoning-dispute-causes-debate-over-definition-of-family/.

[15] www.reinhartlaw.com/Documents/LE_20150413FINAL.pdf?utm_source=Mondaq&utm_medium=syndication&utm_campaign=View-Original.

[16] *Churchless: Understanding Today's Unchurches and How to Connect with Them* by George Barna & David Kinnaman (general editors), Tyndale Momentum (Tyndale House Publishers), 2014 (p. 117).

[17] Barna Group tweet on January 23, 2018, @BarnaGroup.

[18] See illustrations of dysfunctional family situations in the Old Testament, like Cain and Abel, Abraham and Sarah, Lot, Jacob and Esau, Samson, Eli, David with Bathsheba, and Joseph; information about widows in 1 Timothy 5:3-16; widows and orphans in James 1:27; and examples of single people serving the Lord in the NT, like Paul, Timothy, John the Baptist, and Lazarus with Mary and Martha.

[19] *American Psychological Association.* www.apa.org/topics/divorce/.

[20] *ReGenerations: Why Connecting Generations Matter (and how to do it)* by Jessica Stollings, ReGenerations, North Charleston, 2015 (p. 49).

[21] Richard Fry. *Pew Research Center. October 2017.* www.pewresearch.org/fact-tank/2017/10/11/the-share-of-americans-living-without-a-partner-has-increased-especially-among-young-adults/?utm_source=Pew+Research+Center&utm_campaign=a2b9bd68d5-EMAIL_CAMPAIGN_2017_10_11&utm_medium=email&utm_term=0_3e953b9b70-a2b9bd68d5-399502765.

[22] www.healthymarriageinfo.org/.../marriage-facts/download.aspx?id=264.

[23] www.census.gov/hhes/socdemo/marriage/.

[24] Lindy Lowry. *Outreach Magazine.* June 2015. www.outreachmagazine.com/features/4223-the-priority-and-potential-of-single-parent-ministry.html.

[25] *Churchless: Understanding Today's Unchurched and How to Connect with Them,* by George Barna and David Kinnaman, Tyndale House, Carol Stream, 2014 (p. 109).

[26] *Focus on the Family.* www.focusonthefamily.com/socialissues/promos/supreme-court-marriage-decision#summary.

[27] *Churchless: Understanding Today's Unchurched and How to Connect with Them* by George Barna and David Kinnaman, Tyndale House, Carol Stream, 2014 (p. 9).

[28] For example see Kelly Shattuck's article in *Church Leaders:* www.churchleaders.com/pastors/pastor-articles/139575-7-startling-facts-an-up-close-look-at-church-attendance-in-america.html.

[29] *Hartford Institute for Religion Research.* www.hirr.hartsem.edu/research/fastfacts/fast_facts.html#sizecong.

[30] Emma Green. *The Atlantic.* August 2016. www.theatlantic.com/politics/archive/2016/08/religious-participation-survey/496940/.

[31] *Essential Church: Reclaiming a Generation of Dropouts* by Thom S. Rainer and Sam S. Rainer III, B&H Publishing Group, Nashville, 2008 (p. 2).

[32] I take this phrase from the title *The Rise of the Nones: Understanding and Reaching the Religiously Unaffiliated* by James Emery White, published by Baker Books, Grand Rapids, 2014.

[33] *The Next America: Boomers, Millennials, and the Looming Generational Showdown* by Paul Taylor, Public Affairs Books (Perseus Books Group), Philadelphia, 2014.

[34] *The Rise of the Nones: Understanding and Reaching the Religiously Unaffiliated,* by James Emery White, Baker Books, Grand Rapids, 2014 (p. 21).

[35] *They Like Jesus But Not The Church: Insights from Emerging Generations,* by Dan Kimball, Zondervan Publishing, Grand Rapids, 2007 (p. 12).

[36] Cathy Lynn Grossman. *USA Today.* August 2007. http://usatoday30.usatoday.com/news/religion/2007-08-06-church-dropouts_N.htm.

[37] Kyle Smith. *New York Post.* September 2016. http://nypost.com/2016/09/03/millennials-are-totally-mixed-up-about-what-they-believe-in/.

[38] These are my comments – not Bergler's.

[39] *From Here to Maturity: Overcoming the Juvenilization of American Christianity, by Thomas E.* Bergler, Eerdmans, Grand Rapids, 2014 (in Introduction p. xii).

[40] See *The Pastoral Epistles (Revised Edition),* by Homer A. Kent, Jr., Moody Press, Chicago, 1982, (pp. 281-282).

[41] *The MacArthur New Testament Commentary: 2 Timothy* by John MacArthur, Jr., Moody Press, Chicago, 1995 (p. 154).

[42] See Cameron Cole's article on *Preaching.com:* https://www.preaching.com/articles/kids-need-exegetical-bible-teaching-long-haul/.

[43] *Growing Young: 6 Essential Strategies to Help Young People Discover and Love Your Church* by Kara Powell, Jake Mulder, and Brand Griffin, Baker Books, Grand Rapids, 2016 (p. 129).

[44] See *Inter-Generational Youth Ministry: Why a Balanced View of Connecting the Generations is Essential for The Church* by Mel Walker, Overboard Ministries/Vision For Youth Publishing, 2013, (Chapters 1 and 2).

[45] See Ephesians 6:1-4.

[46] See the narrative in Acts 12 and 13.

47 See Acts 12:25-13:1-3.

48 See Acts 13:13.

49 See Acts 15:36-41 and 1 Peter 5:13.

50 See Luke 22:54-62, John 18:15-18, 25-27; then John 21:20-23 and Acts 2:14ff.

51 *Growing Young: 6 Essential Strategies to Help Young People Discover and Love Your Church* by Kara Powell, Jake Mulder, and Brand Griffin, Baker Books, Grand Rapids, 2016 (p. 14).

52 Actually the meaning here is "from infancy." *The MacArthur New Testament Commentary: 2 Timothy* by John MacArthur, Jr., Moody Press, Chicago, 1995 (p. 138).

53 See Matthew 16:18 and Ephesians 3:21.

54 Parents, I understand that recent news stories are headlined by the accounts of sinful adult predators that prey on naïve, innocent children. I hate those accounts as much as you do, and I champion the efforts of churches that are doing all they can to protect the minors who are involved in their ministries. Parents, other significant family members, guardians, legal authorities, and church leaders must collaborate to protect our kids from evil. I would not want my children or grandchildren to be anywhere near a church children's or youth ministry that does not build intensive, legal safeguards into their programs. However, the sinful influences in society do not negate the importance of godly models and examples (see 2 Timothy 3:10 and 14) for our kids.

55 See this narrative in Daniel 3.

56 www.biblestudytools.com/lexicons/hebrew/nas/shachah.html.

57 See Daniel 3:24.

58 *Fuller Youth Institute. 2008.* https://fulleryouthinstitute.org/articles/theological-principles-behind-intergenerational-youth-ministry.

59 See Biblical references such as Acts 11:19-26; Acts 12:1-19; 1 Timothy 5:1-2; 2 Timothy 2:2; 2 Timothy 3:10-17; Titus 2:1-8 as examples of inter-generational connections in the church.

[60] See *The Purpose-Driven Church* (ePub format) by Rick Warren, Zondervan, Grand Rapids, 1995.

[61] For some Biblical references to the church being a body see: Romans 12:4-5; 1 Corinthians 10:17; 1 Corinthians 12:12 and 27; Ephesians 4:12; Ephesians 5:23 and 30; and Colossians 1:24.

[62] Benjamin Kerns. *The reThink Group.* April 2014. http://orangeblogs.org/orangeleaders/2014/04/15/what-happens-when-parents-and-kids-see-youth-group-as-simply-an-elective/.

[63] Benjamin Kerns. *The reThink Group.* April 2014. http://orangeblogs.org/orangeleaders/2014/04/15/what-happens-when-parents-and-kids-see-youth-group-as-simply-an-elective/.

[64] See *Inter-Generational Youth Ministry: Why a Balanced View of Connecting the Generations is Essential for The Church* by Mel Walker, Overboard Ministries/Vision For Youth Publishing, 2013 (Chapter 7, pages 71-92).

[65] For more information on the "family-integrated church" movement see: *A Weed in the Church* by Scott T. Brown, National Center for Family-Integrated Churches, 2011; *Family-Integrated Church* by J. Mark Fox, Xulon Press, 2006; or *Family Driven Faith* by Voddie Baucham, Jr., Crossway Books, 2007.

[66] Note: For more information about Chap Clark's 5 to 1 ratio see: http://billygraham.org/decision-magazine/september-2004/in-spite-of-how-they-act/, www.cpyu.org/2013/08/13/5-adults-to-1-kid-but-who-are-the-5/, http://fulleryouthinstitute.org/articles/moving-away-from-the-kid-table, and http://theparentcue.org/why-your-kids-need-five-other-adults-in-their-lives/.

[67] Chap Clark. *Billy Graham Evangelistic Association.* August 2004. https://billygraham.org/decision-magazine/september-2004/in-spite-of-how-they-act/.

[68] https://twitter.com/RevKevDeYoung/status/930528317073182720.

[69] John Rosemond. *La Crosse Tribune*. January 2017. http://lacrossetribune.com/lifestyles/relationships-and-special-occasions/john-rosemond-your-kids-should-not-be-the-most-important/article_e61f4a20-c15e-53c6-ba51-e86af16ab957.html.

[70] For a revealing take on "Stop Idolizing Your Family" see Francis Chan's challenge at: http://churchleaders.com/pastors/videos-for-pastors/275963-francis-chan-a-challenge-to-the-church.html.

[71] I am referring to my workshops for youth workers at Clarks Summit University's 2017 *Teen Leadership Conference*.

[72] See Matthew 25:14-30.

[73] *You Lost Me: Why Young Christians Are Leaving Church…and Rethinking Faith* by David Kinnaman, Baker Books (Baker Publishing Group), Grand Rapids, 2011 (p. 13).

[74] For one idea of how discipleship could work within the fabric of youth ministry see: *Impacting the Next Generation: A Strategy for Discipleship in Youth Ministry* by Mel Walker, Regular Baptist Press, Schaumburg, 2002.

[75] See Proverbs 3:27.

[76] See *Purpose-Driven Church: Growth Without Compromising Your Message & Mission* by Rick Warren, Zondervan, Grand Rapids, 1995.

[77] Again, see Ephesians 4:11-16.

[78] See definition of the term "nuclear family" in Chapter 2.

[79] *Inter-Generational Youth Ministry: Why a Balanced View of Connecting the Generations is Essential for The Church* by Mel Walker, Overboard Ministries/Vision For Youth Publishing, 2013 (p. 174).

[80] *The MacArthur New Testament Commentary: Matthew 8-15* by John MacArthur, Jr., Moody Publishers, Chicago, 1987 (pp. 230, 232).

[81] *The MacArthur New Testament Commentary: Luke 11-17* by John MacArthur, Jr., Moody Publishers, Chicago, 2013 (pp. 283-284).

[82] See 3 John 4, *"I have no greater joy than to hear that my children walk in truth."*

[83] See Ephesians 6:1-4.

[84] See *Simple Church: Returning to God's Process for Making Disciples* by Thom S. Rainer and Eric Geiger, B&H Publishing Group, Nashville, 2011.

[85] See *Tyranny of the Urgent – Revised & Expanded* by Charles E. Hummel, Inter-Varsity Fellowship, Downers Grove, 1994.

[86] Steve McSwain. *The Huffington Post.* Jaunary 2014. www.huffingtonpost.com/steve-mcswain/why-nobody-wants-to-go-to_b_4086016.html.

[87] *Lasting Impact: 7 Powerful Conversations That Will Help Your Church Grow* by Carey Nieuwhof, The reThink Group, Cumming, 2015 (Conversation #2).

[88] https://albertmohler.com/2016/01/20/the-scandal-of-biblical-illiteracy-its-our-problem-4/.

[89] For example see: www.chron.com/news/article/Census-data-shows-non-traditional-families-are-1849358.php.

[90] See this important post from Dr. Ed Stetzer: www.christianitytoday.com/edstetzer/2015/july/epidemic-of-bible-illiteracy-in-our-churches.html.

[91] See *From Here to Maturity: Overcoming the Juvenilization of American Christianity* by Thomas E. Bergler, William E. Eerdmans Publishing Company, Grand Rapids, 2014.

[92] *The Economist.* March 2009. www.economist.com/node/13216053.

[93] *The Odyssey* by Homer, Harvard University Press, Cambridge, 1976 (p. 53).

[94] *Wuest's Word Studies: The Pastoral Epistles* by Kenneth S. Wuest, Eerdmans Publishing, Grand Rapids, 1952 (p. 191).

[95] See *Mentoring the Next Generation: A Strategy for Connecting the Generations* by Mel Walker, Regular Baptist Press, Arlington, 2003.

[96] For more information about Chap Clark's 5 to 1 ratio see http://billygraham.org/decision-magazine/september-2004/in-spite-of-how-they-act/, www.cpyu.org/2013/08/13/5-adults-to-1-kid-but-who-are-the-5/, http://fulleryouthinstitute.org/articles/moving-away-from-the-kid-table, and http://theparentcue.org/why-your-kids-need-five-other-adults-in-their-lives/.

[97] For more information about how modern culture has segregated the generations read Chapters 1 and 2 in *Inter-Generational Youth Ministry: Why a Balanced View of Connecting the Generations is Essential for The Church* by Mel Walker, Overboard Ministries/Vision For Youth Publishing, 2013.

[98] Authors Neil Howe and William Strauss are widely credited for coining the term "Millennials" – see Samantha Sharf's *Forbes'* article: www.forbes.com/sites/samanthasharf/2015/08/24/what-is-a-millennial-anyway-meet-the-man-who-coined-the-phrase/#b2af5614a053.

[99] Allison McWilliams. *The Huffington Post.* April 2017. www.huffingtonpost.com/entry/get-ready-here-comes-generation-z_us_58e63509e4b0ee31ab95350c.

[100] Jeremy Boudinet. *The Muse.* www.themuse.com/advice/what-millennials-really-need-hint-its-not-feedback and www.huffingtonpost.com/julie-kantor/give-them-what-they-want-_b_8783712.html for example.

[101] *Wuest's Word Studies: The Pastoral Epistles by* Kenneth S. Wuest, Eerdmans Publishing, Grand Rapids, 1952 (p. 191).

[102] See specific statistics and sources of information in Chapter 2.

[103] See 1 Peter 5:8.

[104] This is the author's paraphrase of Acts 11:23.

[105] *Rediscovering Church: The Story and Vision of Willow Creek Community Church* by Lynne and Bill Hybels, Zondervan Publishing House, Grand Rapids, 1995 (p. 169).

[106] *Think Orange: Imagine the Impact When Church & Family Collide* by Reggie Joiner, David C. Cook, Colorado Springs, 2009 (p. 25).

[107] *Partnering With Parents: A Greater Influence Occurs When the Church and Parents Blend Their Efforts Together* article in The Baptist Tribune, November/December 2017, Baptist Bible Fellowship International, Springfield, MO.

[108] See *The DNA of D6: Building Blocks of Generational Discipleship* by Ron Hunter, Jr., Randall House, Nashville, 2015.

[109] See *Partnering with Parents in Youth Ministry: The Practical Guide to Today's Family Based Youth Ministry* by Jim Burns and Mike DeVries, Gospel Light, Ventura, 2015.

[110] See *The Legacy Path: Discover Intentional Spiritual Parenting* by Brian Haynes, Randall House, Nashville, 2011.

[111] See *Inter-Generational Youth Ministry: Why a Balanced View of Connecting the Generations is Essential for The Church* by Mel Walker, Overboard Ministries/Vision For Youth Publishing, 2013 (Chapters 1 and 2).

[112] I make this observation based upon recent pastoral placement calls to the alumni office at the Christian university where I served for almost 20 years.

[113] See Ephesians 4:11-16 and 2 Timothy 3:10-17.

[114] For example see 2 Timothy 3:1-9.

[115] See Acts 1:8.

[116] See *When God Shows Up: A History of Protestant Youth Ministry in America* by Mark Senter III, Baker Academic, Grand Rapids, 2010.

[117] *Transforming Children into Spiritual Campions: Why Children Should be Your Church's #1 Priority* by George Barna, Regal Books (Gospel Light), Ventura, 2003 (p. 33) and www.barna.com/research/evangelism-is-most-effective-among-kids/.

[118] *The Sticky Faith Guide for Your Family: Over 100 Practical Ideas to Build Lasting Faith in Kids* by Dr. Kara Powell, Zondervan, Grand Rapids, 2014 (in Foreword by Dr. Jim Burns).

[119] *The Sticky Faith Guide for Your Family: Over 100 Practical Ideas to Build Lasting Faith in Kids* by Dr. Kara Powell, Zondervan, Grand Rapids, 2014 (quote from Christian Smith and Melissa Lundquist Denton in *Soul Searching*).

[120] See examples in the Bible like Saul (the Apostle Paul) in Acts 9, the Ethiopian eunuch in Acts 8, and the Philippian jailer in Acts 16 of people who came to Christ as adults.

[121] For some further reading on the subject of family ministry in the church, see: *Trained in the Fear of God: Family Ministry in Theological, Historical, and Practical Perspective* by Randy Stinson and Timothy Paul Jones, Kregel Academic & Professional, Grand Rapids, 2011; *A Theology for Family Ministries* by Michael and Michelle Anthony, B&H Academic, Nashville, 2011; and *Perspectives on Family Ministry: 3 Views* by Paul Renfro, Brandon Shields, and Jay Strother, B&H Academic, Nashville, 2009.

[122] *Family Driven Faith: Doing What It Takes to Raise Sons and Daughters Who Walk With God* by Voddie Baucham, Jr., Crossway, Wheaton, 2007 (pp. 198-199).

[123] I have not been able to find the original source of the phrase, "parents are the primary disciplers of their own children." However, for more information on this issue see, *Perspectives on Your Child's Education: 4 Views* by Mark Eckel, G. Tyler Fischer, Troy Temple, and Michael S. Wilder, B&H Academics, Nashville, 2009.

[124] Here is a book that may be the definitive work on helping teenagers assimilate into a local church: *Adoptive Youth Ministry: Integrating Emerging Generations into the Family of Faith* edited by Chap Clark, Baker Academic, Grand Rapids, 2016.

[125] Julie Lythcott-Haims. *Business Insider.* July 2015. www.businessinsider.com/the-rise-of-the-helicopter-parent-2015-7.

[126] http://youthspecialties.com/blog/incorporating-parents-in-youth-ministry/.

[127] For example, see *Engaging Parents as Allies* by Wayne Rice, Standard Pub., Cincinnati, 2009.

[128] See *Partnering with Parents in Youth Ministry* by Jim Burns and Mike DeVries, Gospel Light, Ventura, 2003.

[129] Brian Dembowczyk. *The Gospel Project.* February 2015. www.gospelproject.com/2015/02/04/5-easy-ways-help-parents-discip le-kids/.

[130] See *Think Orange: Imagine the Impact When Church and Family Collide* by Reggie Joiner, David C. Cook, Colorado Springs, 2009.

[131] See *The DNA of D6: Building Blocks of Generational Discipleship* by Ron Hunter, Jr., Randall House, Nashville, 2015.

[132] See *Shift: What It Takes to Finally Reach Families Today* by Brian Haynes, Group Publishing, Loveland, 2009.

[133] See *Family Driven Faith by* Voddie Baucham, Crossway Books, Wheaton, 2007.

[134] See *A Weed in the Church: How a Culture of Age Segregation is Destroying the Younger Generation, Fragmenting the Family, and Dividing the Church* by Scott T. Brown, The National Center for Family-Integrated Churches, Wake Forest, 2010. Another source of information about this viewpoint is: www.dividedthemovie.com/.

[135] See Ephesians 4:11-16 and Ephesians 6:1-4.

[136] See Ephesians 4:12.

[137] See Ephesians 4:11.

[138] *Wuest's Word Studies – Ephesians and Colossians in the Greek New Testament for the English Reader* by Kenneth S. Wuest, Eerdmans Publishing Company, Grand Rapids, 1953 (p. 101).

[139] See Philippians 2:5-11.

[140] *Family-Based Youth Ministry: Reaching the Been-There, Done-That Generation* by Mark DeVries, Inter-Varsity Press, Downers Grove, 1994.

[141] See Proverbs 11:14; 15:22; 24:6.

[142] David Mathis. *Desiring God.* January 2012. www.desiringgod.org/articles/parents-beware-proverbs-are-not-promises.

[143] David Mathis. *Desiring God.* January 2012. www.desiringgod.org/articles/parents-beware-proverbs-are-not-promises.

[144] See 2 Timothy 3:16-17; 2 Peter 1:21; and Hebrews 4:12.

[145] See passages like 2 Corinthians 7.

[146] *Already Gone: Why Your Kids Will Quit Church and What You Can Do To Stop It* by Ken Ham, Master Books, Green Forest, 2009 (Chapter 1).

[147] For some helpful information on this subject, see Walt Muller's post at: https://cpyu.org/2013/05/16/inside-the-teen-brain/.

[148] Ryan Nelson. *Faithlife.* July 2015. https://blog.faithlife.com/blog/2015/07/the-prince-of-preachers-has-something-to-say-to-church-shoppers/.

[149] See passages like: Matthew 16:18; Acts 20:28; Ephesians 2:20 and4:11; 1 Timothy 3:15; Hebrews 10:25; 1 Peter 5:1-2; and Revelation 1:11.

[150] See *Why We Love the Church: In Praise of Institutions & Organized Religions* by Kevin DeYoung and Ted Kluck, Moody Publishers, Chicago, 2009 (pp. 73-74).

[151] This article by Kami Gilmour from *ChurchLeaders* may be an encouragement to parents on this topic: https://churchleaders.com/youth/youth-leaders-articles/312872-holding-on-to-hope-12-truths-for-parents-whose-kids-wander-away-from-faith.html?utm_source=youth-weekly-nl&utm_medium=email&utm_content=text-link&utm_content=text-link&utm_campaign=youth-weekly-nl&maropost_id=742275991&mpweb=256-5133551-742275991.

152 Don Koller. *Youth Specialties*. December 2017.
https://youthspecialties.com/blog/3-reasons-students-dont-engage/?
_cldee=bWVssd2Fsa2VyQGVwaXgubmV0&recipientid=contact-6c2623
9748c1e41181bd000c296f8bc0-92b31b4c9cbc403597bb000d3b057ea4&ut
m_source=ClickDimensions&utm_medium=email&utm_campaign=20
17%20YS%20Weekly&esid=2673522d-88da-e711-82bc-000c296f8bc0.

153 Jonathan Mansur. *The Gospel Coalition*. July 2015.
www.thegospelcoalition.org/article/4-types-parental-involvement-stu
dent-ministry. (See also: *Perspectives on Your Child's Education: 4 Views*
by Mark Eckel, G. Tyler Fischer, Troy Temple and Michael Wilder, B&H
Publishing Group, Nashville, 2009 (p. 55).

154 *The Word Study Concordance* by George V. Wigram and Ralph D.
Winter, William Carey Library, Pasadena, 1978 (pp. 466-468).

155 See Luke 14:27 and John 8:31.

156 See
https://bible.org/seriespage/2-understanding-meaning-term-disciple
.

157 David Briggs. *The Huffington Post*. October 2014.
www.huffingtonpost.com/david-briggs/the-no-1-reason-teens-kee_b_
6067838.html.

158 https://lifewayresearch.com/2007/08/07/parents-churches-
can-help-teens-stay-in-church/.

159 For example, see 2 Peter 3:18, *"But grow in grace, and in the knowledge
of our Lord and Savior Jesus Christ."*

160 See Acts 16:1-5.

161 See *Inter-Generational Youth Ministry: Why a Balanced View of
Connecting the Generations is Essential for The Church* by Mel Walker,
Overboard Ministries/Vision For Youth Publishing, 2013 (Chapter 2).

162 Greg Stier. *Dare 2 Share*. March 2016.
http://gregstier.dare2share.org/the-hidden-danger-in-dropping-yout
h-ministry-for-a-family-ministry-approach.

[163] *Barna Group.* October 2004.
www.barna.com/research/evangelism-is-most-effective-among-kids/ and

[164] Greg Stier. *ChurchLeaders.* October 2016.
https://churchleaders.com/outreach-missions/outreach-missions-articles/288607-shocking-message-gospel-hope-reaching-increasingly-anti-christian-culture.html.

[165] Justin Taylor. *The Gospel Coalition.* May 2011.
https://blogs.thegospelcoalition.org/justintaylor/2011/05/16/new-testament-metaphors-for-the-church/.

[166] See the following passages that refer to the church as the "bride of Christ" – 2 Corinthians 11:2; Ephesians 5:31-32; Revelation 19:7-9; and Revelation 21:9.

[167] See the following passages that refer to the church as the "body of Christ" – Romans 12:4-5; 1 Corinthians 10:17, 12:12, 12:27; Ephesians 4:14, 5:23, 5:30.

[168] See the following passages that refer to the church as "God's house" – Ephesians 2:19-22 and 1 Peter 2:5.

[169] See the following passages that refer to the church as the "family or household of God" – Matthew 12:49-50; 2 Corinthians 6:18; Galatians 6:10; Ephesians 2:19; and 1 Timothy 5:1.

[170] See *Dictionary of Biblical Imagery: An Encyclopedic Exploration of the Images, Symbols, Motifs, Metaphors, Figures of Speech and Literary Patterns of the Bible*, editors: Leland Ryken, James C. Wilhoit, Tremper Longman III, Inter-Varsity Press, Downers Grove, 1998 (pp. 14-15).

[171] See the following passages that refer to our "adoption" into God's family – Romans 8:15, 23, 9:4; Galatians 4:5; and Ephesians 1:5.

[172] *Adopted into God's Family: Exploring a Pauline Metaphor (New Studies in Biblical Theology)* by Trevor Burke, IVP Academic, Downers Grove, 2006.

[173] See Acts 13:9.

[174] www.lyricsondemand.com/tvthemes/cheerslyrics.html.

[175] Benjamin Kerns. *The reThink Group.* April 2014. http://orangeblogs.org/orangeleaders/2014/04/15/what-happens-when-parents-and-kids-see-youth-group-as-simply-an-elective/.

[176] I am borrowing the phrase "family unfriendly" from Mortimer B. Zuckerman's 2007 article from *U.S. News & World Re*port: www.usnews.com/opinion/mzuckerman/articles/2007/10/05/editorial.

[177] See Conversation #7 in this book.

[178] I am also borrowing the phrase "family-friendly" from *The Family Friendly Church* by Ben Freudenburg, with Rick Lawrence, Group Publishing (Vital Ministry), Loveland, 1998.

[179] See *The Post-Church Christian: Dealing with the Generational Baggage of Our Faith* by Paul Nyquist and Carson Nyquist, Moody Publishers, Chicago, 2013.

[180] For example see: *Youth Ministry in a Post-Christian World: A Hopeful Wake-Up Call* by Brock Morgan, The Youth Cartel, San Diego, 2013.

[181] Ed Stetzer. *Christianity Today.* July 2014. www.christianitytoday.com/edstetzer/2014/july/power-of-invitation-our-god-pursues-lost-and-so-should-we.html.

[182] Here is a helpful article for church leaders from Thom Rainer in *Christianity Today*: www.christianitytoday.com/edstetzer/2014/july/power-of-invitation-our-god-pursues-lost-and-so-should-we.html.

[183] See *Inter-Generational Youth Ministry: Why a Balanced View of Connecting the Generations is Essential for the Church* by Mel Walker, Overboard Ministries/Vision For Youth Publishing, 2013 (Chapters 1 and 2).

[184] See http://nfpaonline.org/page-1105741 for the history of foster care in the United States.

[185] See www.bbbs.org/history/.

[186] www.tlc.com/tv-shows/long-lost-family/.

[187] See also Matthew 28:19-20 and James 1:22.

[188] Karl Vaters. *Christianity Today.* January 2018. www.christianitytoday.com/karl-vaters/2018/january/recalibrate-10-steps-church-this-year-dead-decade.html?start=1.

[189] For example see: Matthew 25:14-30.

[190] See https://en.wikipedia.org/wiki/Durban.

[191] https://simple.wikipedia.org/wiki/Child-headed_family.

[192] Matthew 22:37-39.

[193] See 1 Thessalonians 2:10-12.

[194] See Proverbs 3:5-6; John 15:5, and Titus 2:11-13.

[195] See Deuteronomy 6:4.

[196] *The MacArthur New Testament Commentary, 1 Timothy* by John MacArthur, Moody Press, Chicago, 1995 (p. 164).

[197] *The Pastoral Epistles* by Homer A. Kent, Jr., Moody Press, Chicago, 1982, (p. 280).

[198] See *The Pastoral Epistles* by Homer A. Kent, Jr., Moody Press, Chicago, 1982, (introduction).

[199] *The Practice of Godliness* by Jerry Bridges, NavPress/Tyndale House Publishers, Colorado Springs, 2008 (Chapter 1).

[200] See http://time.com/4361866/adulting-definition-meaning/.

[201] For example, one such result is: Jacquelle Crowe's article from *Desiring God:* www.desiringgod.org/articles/adulting-to-the-glory-of-god.

[202] See again Ephesians 3:15 and Ephesians 6:4.

[203] See *The Juvenilization of American Christianity* by Thomas E. Bergler, William E. Eerdmans Publishing Company, Grand Rapids, MI, 2012 and *From Here to Maturity: Overcoming the Juvenilization of American Christianity,* by Thomas E. Bergler, William E. Eerdmans Publishing Company, Grand Rapids, MI, 2014.

[204] Drew Dyck's interview with Thomas Bergler:
www.christianitytoday.com/ct/2015/januaryfebruary/its-time-for-church-to-grow-up.html.

[205] *Barna Group.* October 2014.
www.barna.com/research/evangelism-is-most-effective-among-kids/.

[206] For instance see Philippians 2:25 and 2 Peter 1:5-11.

[207] See Romans 8:29 and 2 Corinthians 3:18.

[208] For further study on the life of Timothy in the Bible read: Acts 16:1-3 (also Acts 14:1-7, 21); 17:14-15; 18:5; 20:4; Romans 16:21; 1 Corinthians 4:17; 2 Corinthians 1:1, 19; Philippians 1:1; 2:19-24; 1 Thessalonians 3:2; Philemon 1; Hebrews 13:23; and the Epistles of 1 and 2 Timothy.

[209] See 1 Timothy 4:12, *"Let no one despise your youth, but be an example to the believers in word, conduct, in love, in spirit, in faith, in purity."*

Made in the USA
Columbia, SC
26 June 2018